YEHUDI MENUHIN MUSIC GUIDES

Musicology

YEHUDI MENUHIN MUSIC GUIDES

Available
Violin and viola by Yehudi Menuhin and William Primrose
Piano by Louis Kentner
Clarinet by Jack Brymer
Oboe by Leon Goossens and Edwin Roxburgh
Percussion by James Holland

In preparation
contributions on
Bassoon by William Waterhouse
'Cello by William Pleeth
Flute by James Galway
Guitar and lute by Narciso Yepes
Harpsicord and early keyboard instruments by Igor Kipnis
Horn by Barry Tuckwell
Organ by Simon Preston
Trombone by Alan Lumsden
Trumpet by Sidney Ellison
Tuba by John Fletcher
Voice edited by Keith Falkner

YEHUDI MENUHIN MUSIC GUIDES

Musicology

A practical guide

Denis Stevens

SCHIRMER BOOKS
A Division of Macmillan Publishing Co., Inc.
NEW YORK

Copyright © 1980 by Denis Stevens

Schirmer Books
A Division of Macmillan Publishing Co., Inc.
866 Third Avenue, New York, N.Y. 10022

First American Edition 1981

Library of Congress Catalog Card Number: 81-5623

Printed in the United States of America

printing number

1 2 3 4 5 6 7 8 9 10

Library of Congress Cataloging in Publication Data

Stevens, Denis
    Musicology: a practical guide.

    (Yehudi Menuhin music guides)
    Includes index.
    1. Musicology.   I. Title.   II. Series.
    ML3797.S8   780'.01   81-5623
    ISBN 0-02-872540-9   AACR2
    ISBN 0-02-872530-1 (pbk.)

for Leocadia

Tu calamos inflare leves,
ego dicere versus

Contents

Part Three
Applied Musicology

List of Illustrations

Editor's Introduction

Today the field of musicological research and revelation expands in ever-widening circles – its scope constantly reaching into ever more remote areas and eras. The old adventure of treasure search, even of piratical plunder, has evolved into the research and revelation of our contemporary scholars.

In this book Denis Stevens, both scholar and artist (originally an excellent professional violinist – a fact in which I take vicarious pride and comfort), gives us a wonderful insight – urbane, humorous, elegant and fascinating – into the working of musicology. In a way it resembles archaeology in that its art consists of piecing together with infinite patience and intuition every possible scrap of evidence; however, unlike the case of archaeology, the final evidence, if there be such a thing, is enacted through a medium totally different from that of those pieces of evidence themselves.

For example, an archaeologist, grubbing about among his shards and precious rubble, searching for the missing fragments which, when discovered, may complete the ravishing necklace, the splendid statue, the exquisite vase, is driven by the vision of the whole artefact being exhibited in all its once-lost perfection. However, with the musicologist, the result is more elusive and altogether less concrete for the final test lies in the ear of the listener, not in the eye of the beholder. For he is dealing with sounds — sounds which we may never have heard and which, therefore, have to be judged by a set of values which are not simply plastic and aesthetic but are flowing like the current of a river, volatile, ethereal and always subject to the performance, victims of the interpretation.

Denis Stevens has, by dint of indefatigable searchings, be it in the seclusion of great monasteries, libraries or at his own desk, developed and elaborated a unique style, at one and the same time both scholarly and yet alive in the writing of which the sound is essence. How much ancient music has been fated to remain academically pinned to the parchment like some dead and lovely butterfly. It is Stevens' particular gift that his music flies, moves along the stream and strophe of tone as the composers intended and he has achieved this monumental task of shaking the dust from the printed page by training choirs and musicians, conducting performances for audiences who have been moved, quite literally transported into little-known realms, into long-gone ages, into other climes and conditions by the music he has brought to life.

The phenomenon of *recognition* – of recognising the inevitable truth of something, be it a phrase, musical, verbal or written, or a line drawn, is the same universal one which guides the hand of the artist or the inner ear and vision of its creator – even the same echoing in the minds of an audience which leaves no doubt when they have witnessed or heard a supreme manifestation of dance, song, poetry or painting, of that transformation of body and soul when dedicated to and triumphant in the expression of some total demand – a demand requiring inspiration and the joint efforts of diligence and intellect, therefore, of artist as well as scholar.

No effort is too big or too small if it adds one iota to the rightness of a statement. Can it be that this recognition of rightness is something we carry within us, part of our very cells, enabling us intuitively and logically to ferret out that pure evidence of truth in whatever material or situation to which we may direct our attention? Or is it wholly an attribute of the object itself – possessed of its own share of universal truth? Or is it, as in the great discoveries of science, a miraculous moment of magnetism when the essential truth and the searching mind suddenly connect?

The history of the arts and sciences is a field strewn with the bones of battles fought against entrenched ideas, stale prejudices, hierarchical emnity and sheer mental and moral laziness. I am full of admiration for those scholarly soldiers whose lively minds never tire of the fight and whose battle-cry might well be: 'For I will overturn, over-turn, overturn it, until he (the new and fresh idea) come whose right it is and I will give it him'; give it us, to all those whose lives have benefitted from the exhausting spadework, the passionate application of that breed who are never satisfied with the accepted.

It has been my good fortune to have enjoyed the collab-oration and the practical advice of Denis Stevens for many years. Unfailingly good-natured and balanced, he has instilled in me a deep respect, as well as a profound gratitude for musicology, not least for himself in particular. This the reader will well understand as he progresses through this book which, to my way of thinking, performs the positively acrobatic intellectual feat of being both erud-ite and translucent – surely unique among most scholarly works.

YEHUDI MENUHIN
1980

Author's Preface

If, over the years, a single *ostinato* has dominated my thoughts about music, it is this: the possibility of writing a book on 'applied musicology', as it has sometimes been described by friends and colleagues who have urged me to bring it to completion. During those years, I have often had the opportunity of discussing the interaction of music and scholarship with Yehudi and Diana Menuhin, whose good counsel and warm encouragement on so many occasions helped me to work out an approach to the topic that could prove valuable to musicians. I shall always remain grateful for their constant and loyal support in transforming an idea into reality. Special thanks must go to Eric Fenby for his continuing interest and enthusiasm, as well as for his invaluable comments on the book in its initial stages. At Macdonald's editorial offices, Penelope Hoare and Alice Clark never lacked kindness and patience despite the demands of a fastidious author. My greatest debt, however, is to my wife – the dedicatee of this book – without whose love and inspiration I would never have completed my task.

D.S.

Part One

Viewpoints

One
Music and Musicology –
A Personal Approach

> The old-fashioned image of the dry-as-dust, scholarly musicologist . . . is no longer valid.
>
> Yehudi Menuhin: *Musicology vs. Performance*

This is not a book for musicologists: they already know it all. Yet their image has been changing slowly in recent years, and they have begun to show a real concern for what is happening in the world of performance, as well as try to reach out and persuade members of the younger generation to give good music the chance that it deserves in the face of highly commercialized noise and vulgarity. But the typical scholar is often reluctant to give way to his innermost feelings. Although well-equipped with practical as well as recondite knowledge, he is rarely able to venture forth to offer counsel and guidance to the teeming throng of instrumentalists, singers, conductors – hungry for knowledge and thirsting for second knowledge – for the simple reason that he is too busy serving on committees and sub-committees, publishing in order not to perish, programming computers, applying for grants, and (of course) teaching – which consumes an immoderate amount of time if it is to be properly and conscientiously carried out.

Until the situation improves, this book may prove to be of some assistance to those who believe that a little knowledge, though potentially dangerous, is better than none at all, especially in the quicksands and quagmires of musicology. For as long as I can remember, I have been passionately attached to music – the Cinderella of the arts – and to her step-sister, musicology; and even as a teen-age violinist I tended to neglect Ševčík in favour of Grove's Dictionary, though I would never miss the chance to play chamber music or in an orchestra, especially if there were young ladies in attendance. I could sing, play and listen to music, but until I read about it in some detail its nature, form and *raison d'être* persistently eluded me. I found then, as I still find, that certain kinds of extremely useful knowledge are frequently half-hidden or completely stifled by unsatisfactory organization of material, a dull, contorted and unimaginative literary style, and a desire to impress the reader without really satisfying his curiosity. The foregoing might well pass as a working definition for much musicological writing of the more cabbalistic type, in which the overburdened and possibly over-qualified author is writing for his own pleasure and possibly that of two or three others incautious enough to invade his pet preserve; yet the fact remains that beneath the awesome mound of chaff there are usually a few precious grains of wheat.

I make no apology for the obvious bias in the pages that follow, for the predominance of instrumental volumes in the Yehudi Menuhin Music Guides tempted me to redress the balance very slightly by allocating as much space as possible to the peculiar problems of vocal music, especially in the centuries prior to the age of Bach and Handel. The recent enthusiasm for early music is also much bound up with instrumental participation, which though admirable in its own way can sometimes blind us to the fact that so far nobody has been able to market a do-it-yourself voice kit. If my discussions of *musica ficta*, barring, text underlay, liturgy, vocal colour and ornamentation bring some comfort and assistance to those who find such matters difficult to deal with, I shall feel that something useful has been accomplished, even though further information may ultimately be required. To this end, I have mentioned in the body of the text some articles, books and editions that seem to offer help of the right kind. The fact that a work is not mentioned, however, does not imply that it might not prove useful. The plain fact is that to cover such a vast area of knowledge with any degree of success one would have to envisage a multi-volume work in a much larger format. And this must be a project for the future.

Quite clearly, then, no space can be set aside for a consideration of music and musicology of the non-western world, nor can I offer instruction on the manufacture and technique of replicas of early instruments. Those desiring to know how to play the racket in ten easy lessons should look elsewhere for aid and succour; and those who pine for a chapter on 'They laughed when I sat down to the shag-bolt' must needs remain equally disappointed. A few months' zealous application should suffice to assure competence in the playing of most instruments dating from before the 18th century, and detailed tutors are not in short supply. But the budding performer who wishes to develop his knowledge and control of the vast accumulation of musicological materials simply cannot expect to achieve his aim and object in a few months: indeed he might try to avoid early disillusionment by thinking in terms of not a few years. This book, intended to be a highly concentrated Baedeker-type guide through the thickets and pitfalls of musical scholarship and its practical application (especially in earlier repertory), supplies some direct information but a larger amount of indirect information – or 'second knowledge'.

The need for such assistance was first brought to my attention when, as a post-graduate student at Oxford after World War II, I found myself involved in the business of providing incidental music to plays by Elizabethan and Jacobean dramatists produced by the OUDS, or re-activating the Opera Club, or beginning what eventually grew to be a long-term association with the BBC: especially the Third Programme and Radio 3, but in addition the Transcription Service, Television, European, and Overseas services. 'Authentic' music of one kind or another was constantly in demand; moreover there were, in the early 1950s, a number of highly gifted exponents of early instruments such as the harpsichord, baroque organ, recorder, lute, viols. The era of the krummhorn, racket, sackbut and nakers had yet to dawn, but nevertheless our broadcasts and concerts – which were motivated primarily by the quality and interest of the music, and only secondarily by considerations of tone-colour – lapped us in soft Lydian airs, smooth and gentle sounds, and a distinct feeling of being present at the birth of a new age in early music, as in fact it turned out to be.

As a BBC producer, I would receive letters objecting to this or that consort, though it was obvious even at the time that listeners had not had the opportunity of training their ears to accept such strange sounds. And there were those who wrote letters asking what a counter-tenor really looked like, and did he have hair on his face? Even critics, most of them full of wonder and enthusiasm, occasionally expressed puzzlement at some of the more abstruse mathematical concepts in medieval music, such as the isorhythm; whereupon a spirited supporter would quickly reply that if a listener or a critic is prepared to devote some intellectual effort to the comprehension of the more complex of 20th-century scores, he can surely, out of fairness and justice, brighten up his grey matter with a little coloured notation or equate the subtleties of *color* and *talea* with the demands of twelve-note technique. However different they may be as compositional methods, they are both essentially products of disciplined minds.

Since those distant days the situation has greatly changed. No longer is there any need to fight for early music, as it has now been thoroughly accepted and assimilated by an apparently insatiable public. But the balance is sometimes faulty, in that there is too much concentration on the pseudo-antique quaintness of bizarre instruments, dozens of them being played by one person, so that we experience variety at the expense of quality and too little concern for what ultimately counts: the music itself. We often find ourselves subjected nowadays to a recital of deservedly obscure and certainly inferior compositions (doubtless photocopied from some serendipitous collection of fourth-rate *Denkmäler*) whose sole claim for resuscitation is that they serve as 'vehicles' for variegated instrumental consorts. I once heard a 'performance' of Isaac's *Missa Carminum* in Venice, and remember with some surprise that a work I had hitherto imagined to have been scored for choral resources could at least make a bold pretence of survival when performed by a solo vocal quartet and a mass of doubling instruments that, placed end to end, would easily have stretched all the way from the Doge's Palace to the Arsenal. More recently, a newly-formed 'consort of early music' has presented programmes of commendable variety but with a far too limited array of participants – twelve instruments played by four musicians, aided by two solo voices. With this severely limited combination they have essayed not only the music of Josquin, which is largely choral in texture, but even some of the great occasional motets by Dufay, written for state ceremonies, dedications of churches, weddings and the like. As originally performed, these works demanded full choral resources accompanied by a group of perhaps half-a-dozen instruments, in a proportion of four singers to one player. But the versions I heard were exactly reversed, with instrumental sound dominating and the 'choral' part reduced to a soprano-tenor duet.

If this kind of treatment were accorded to the Mozart *Requiem*, or Verdi's *Requiem*, or Bach's *Mass in B minor*, the outcry would be long and vehement. And if Schubert's *Octet* were to be performed and recorded without the horn and viola parts, revolution would follow. But when a vocal 'octet' in the form of a double-choir Magnificat by Monteverdi is twice published, twice recorded, and subjected to innumerable executions without the second alto and second bass parts, nobody turns a hair! It is an almost unbelievable state of affairs. Editors, proof-readers, scholars, singers, conductors, critics – they all fall for it, as do the cheering and unsuspecting audiences. All of which goes to show that there is one law for the classics, another for the pre-classics. The former exacts heavy penalties for what it might well choose to call a felony, while the latter scarcely pays attention to what might only be a minor misdemeanour. After all, provided the mutilated carcass is suitably decorated with reproductions of early instruments, nothing can possibly be wrong.

But it is wrong, and it must and should be put right. A fair number of books in several languages exist solely for the purpose of guiding musicians in the interpretation of 17th and 18th-century music, which is in fact not too difficult or abstruse a field. All that has to be decided can be summed up under four main headings: (1) tempo; (2) dynamics; (3) bowing, fingering, phrasing; (4) ornamentation. Of these four, the first three belong rightly to the area of musical commonsense, while only the last calls for detailed research in some suitable chart of ornamentation. Even then, the choice can be fairly wide, for manuscript evidence proves that compositions were subject to widely different ornamental treatment, as so much depended on the kind of instrument, the competence (or otherwise) of the performer, and possibly the building in which they were situated.

Unfortunately for the performer matters are considered in quite another light by the musicologists. Having all leaned more or less in one direction for several decades in so far as the French overture style and *notes inégales* are concerned, some of them are now tired of this boring position and have assumed an almost precisely opposite one, replacing a rigidity of interpretation for a freer and more imaginative attitude. Those able to afford the sum of £31.40 (or the bus fare to a wealthy library) will be able to study the latest fashion in Frederick Neumann's *Ornamentation in Baroque and post-Baroque Music, with Special Emphasis on J.S. Bach* (Princeton, 1979). Here, the rigid and simplified laws for ornamentation codified by previous generations of scholars are now seriously challenged by an impressive mound of evidence derived from primary sources, the result of which is to show that there was no such thing as a common practice in the 17th and 18th centuries.

Techniques and styles were often limited to regional and national areas, rarely passing across those artificial though almost impenetrable boundaries which saw to it, among other things, that there never could be a common spoken language nor a common system of currency in Europe as it then stood.

So, a new book comes along and upsets all prior theories; and possibly in twenty years' time the same kind of thing could happen again.* Research never remains totally immobile. Musicologists, on the other hand, are extremely mobile and they are rarely content until they have tracked down the most obscure source in the most inaccessible library. In this way the sum total of knowledge about a given subject can be much modified over the course of a very few years, and this almost invariably means a loosening rather than a tightening of the reins. After beginning the trills of Bach and Handel on the upper auxiliary note, you may now begin them on the main note. But what is this compared with the falsification of an entire form, or the omission of entire voice-parts, or nonsensical texts for *non sequitur* rondeaux?

In contrast to the multitude of books, articles, and theories about the Baroque and post-Baroque, there is precious little available on the 19th century repertoire (and a thorough study of such a topic would require an entire volume, at the very least), nor is there anything in the way of a reference book that covers the very difficult and complicated music from plainchant to the close of the Renaissance. Because it is manifestly impossible to deal with everything in a book of necessarily limited size and scope, I have decided to offer help where it is most needed – the area sometimes referred to as pre-classical.

Mea culpa: it was not necessary to wait for twenty years. As this book goes to press, I am reading a fascinating musico-philosophical article largely, but by no means exclusively, devoted to the over-dotting problem, in *Musicology V* published by the Musicological Society of Australia, 1979. The author, Graham Pont, has chosen as his title 'A Revolution in the Science and Practice of Music', and to judge by the research contained in 66 closely-filled pages (not to mention 198 footnotes) it will now be essential to re-assess the entire matter. If I may be forgiven the pun, it is almost enough to drive one dotty.

Nevertheless, an attempt such as I have made here to provide a modest degree of guidance through the repertory of the Middle Ages, Renaissance, and Baroque will, I trust, be accepted in the spirit in which it is offered. I propound no hard-and-fast rules. But I insist that due attention be paid to questions of form and content, text and music, sound and sense; for it is upon these matters, in the main, that a successful realization is based. Not all the fancy décor in the world can mask a wrong note, nor can it excuse a fumbling after *ficta* that would disgrace a ten-year-old. Basics must come first. Once that principle is fully understood, the pre-classical confusion will begin to clear up and performances will benefit enormously.

Two

What Is Musicology?

> 'When I use a word,' Humpty-Dumpty said, in a rather scornful tone, 'it means just what I choose it to mean – neither more nor less.'
> Lewis Carroll: *Through the Looking-Glass*

'Musicology' means different things to different musicologists. Even the acceptance of the term met with initial opposition from purists who looked askance at latter-day combinations of Greek roots. But 'music' and 'ology' (which oddly enough was the title of a lecture given in America by Dom Anselm Hughes in the 1930s) mix together in a manner infinitely more convincing than 'corsetorama' or 'talkathon', and they express jointly what may be considered a brief and accurate definition of this particular pursuit – speech, discourse, or learning about music.

It is only when the skeletal definition is fleshed out that one runs into the kind of trouble caused by everybody speaking at the same time. If musicology must include historiography, theory, criticism, ethnocentricity, acoustics, soundscapes, bibliography, stemmatics, watermarkitis and computeromania, one might be forgiven for indulging in specious semantics and explaining the term as a gathering of musics, as if the 'ology' were derived not from λόγος but from the closely related λέγω, as in the word 'anthology'.

Whether bouquet or discourse, musicology in fact if not in name began with the theorists and writers of Greek

11

antiquity, among whom Aristides Quintilianus divided music into science and technique on the one hand, and composition and execution on the other. Boethius, in transferring Greek ideas to the culture of the Christian west, added important material of his own, notably the concept that music is related to morality as well as to science, and that music belongs to the *quadrivium* of mathematical learning as it was understood in the sixth century A.D. Developed in monastic and academic schools throughout Europe, the scientific study of music grew up alongside the many flourishing schools of composition, and there is more than ample proof that theory and practice frequently affected each other on many different levels of comprehension.

Indeed, a few outstanding theorists were also capable composers, just as some famous composers achieved further renown in their capacity as writers about music. Johannes Tinctoris, Lionel Power, Gioseffo Zarlino, Vincenzo Galilei, Thomas Morley, Michael Praetorius, and many representatives of later periods belong to one or other of these categories. At first there was little concern about the history of music, for creative artists and commentators alike thrived upon the music of their own time, having minimal if any access to the work of previous composers. Exceptions there were, of course, but one finds that even in these cases much mystification existed. Zarlino tells us in his *Sopplimenti musicali* (p.18) that he owned an ancient manuscript – presumably of Italian music – whose cover (of later date than the contents) was dated 1397; and that Gioseffo Guami of Lucca sent him similar evidences of what we now call *ars nova* music, without either of them being able to understand what it was all about.

It was not until the 18th century that musical historiography emerged clearly as a branch of the art worthy of serious consideration, but thanks to G.B. Martini, Antonio Eximeno, Charles Burney, John Hawkins and their followers, a solid foundation was laid for future research. Forkel, Ambros, Fétis, Riemann carried the work many stages further, each building to some extent on the work of previous authors, yet adding newly discovered facts and freshly fabricated opinions of his own. Their procedure was still not scientific, nor could it be as long as they were dealing with history – which presupposes a method of selection in which personal whims and prejudices play a not unimportant role.

It may well be that Friedrich Chrysander is best known today for his contributions to Handel research and the old Handel edition, but he also deserves to be remembered for having first employed the term 'musical science' in his *Jahrbücher für musikalische Wissenschaft* (1863, 1867) as a scholarly ideal, through which musical research would emulate that of the realm of pure science by its attention to accuracy and exhaustive study. When Chrysander joined Philipp Spitta and Guido Adler in a quarterly magazine devoted to musicology in 1885 *(Vierteljahrsschrift für Musikwissenschaft)* the same term was used by Adler in his inaugural essay on the 'Scope, Method, and Object of Musical Science'.

Dividing his subject in two sections, historical and systematic, Adler regards the first as a study of musical history, palaeography, forms, theories, and instruments; and the second as an investigation of the laws of music as related to harmony, rhythm, and melody, along with musical psychology and aesthetics, pedagogics, and folklore. Each and every one of these branches would be informed by other sciences outside the domain of music, so that musicologists would be required to have a certain knowledge of general history, palaeography, chronology, diplomatics, bibliography, library and archival methods, literature and languages, liturgiology, mime and dance, biography, acoustics, mathematics, physiology, psychology, logic, grammar, metrics and poetics, pedagogy, aesthetics, and anything else that might seem appropriate.

If all this strikes the reader as a great deal to ask of one man in one lifetime, then let him think twice before he forsakes his instrument to 'become' a musicologist, for the training is long and arduous while the problem of keeping up-to-date with new information becomes increasingly difficult as the years go by and musicological productivity grows at an ever more rapid rate. Detailed accounts of different approaches to the categorization of musical research may be found in 'The Development of Modern Musicology' by Ernst C. Krohn (in *Historical Musicology* by Lincoln Bunce Spiess, New York, 1963, pp. 153-172), and in the lengthy article by Walter Wiora, Hans Albrecht and Hans Hasse in *Die Musik in Geschichte und Gegenwart*, Vol. 9.*

It should be noted, together with all the varied interpretations of the word 'musicology', that words other than *Musikwissenschaft* occur frequently in German works of reference having to do with scholarship in music. One of these in *Musikforschung* (musical research), used not only in the title of journals (*Die Musikforschung, Archiv für Musikforschung*) but also as the name of a society (*Gesellschaft für Musikforschung*). The other term is *Musikgeschichte* (history of music), found in titles such as *Musikgeschichte in Bildern*, a series of volumes devoted to the iconographical aspect of music history. The three principal terms may be seen in titles of periodicals in other languages: *Belgisch Tijdschrift voor Muziekwetenschap; Svensk Tidskrift för Musikforskning; Tijdschrift der Vereeniging voor Nederlandse Muziekgeschiedenis.*

How can a performer hope to find a path through this musicological maze, grasp at the information that is so urgently needed, and extract from it precisely what is wanted and no more? It is easy enough, of course, to consult a dictionary in one's own language, but there is no guarantee that any one dictionary will give all the right answers, and to test the truth of this remark one need only compare entries on the same topic or person in three or four different dictionaries to realize that the divergences can sometimes be alarming. In addition to basic information, a dictionary often gives references to specialized books and

*See also Roland Jackson: *Research Activities in Music* (in progress).

articles in the bibliography. These in turn open up a whole new field of research, not without its attendant problems and frustrations.

'Knowledge,' said Dr Samuel Johnson, 'is of two kinds. We know a subject ourselves, or we know where we can find information upon it'. This 'second knowledge', recognized as being of major importance two centuries ago, ranks nowadays as the only possible answer to the so-called 'information explosion' which has provided such a wealth of research materials that humanity – or rather the humanities – can no longer cope with it. Whereas the sciences and medicine, heavily funded and generously endowed, have been able to devote vast sums of money to the regular publication of indexes and abstracts from books and periodicals in many languages, the humanities (among which music is generally included) have done noticeably less well. That this is due to lack of adequate funds must strike the reader as obvious, since the art of music has always been regarded as a luxury or a soft option, making financial support a matter for active and continuous campaigning, whereas in medicine and science a constant flow of funds reaches organizations almost without their having to ask for it.

Although the *Music Index* and the more recent publications of *RILM* (Répertoire International de la Littérature Musicale) have provided noteworthy assistance, it is a case of 'too little, too late' since there is such a vast backlog of material that only a colossal application of personnel and finance could remedy the situation. The four barriers of distance, language, time and discipline would have to be broken down before any significant advance were made in the field of musical 'second knowledge'. Yet this could be done with comparative ease by applying to musical literature what has already been successfully applied to science and technology. One major problem is that contributions to dictionaries and other works of reference may be made by inadequate as well as by reliable scholars. How then can a novice separate the wheat from the chaff? How distinguish between reliable research and sloppy scholarship?

Fortunately there is a way, albeit a time-consuming one, rather closely related to the now commonly-used method of distilling the quintessence of a masterpiece by comparing carefully several different recorded interpretations – a method now raised to the status of respectability by the publication of proceedings of a congress on that topic at Darmstadt: *Vergleichende Interpretationskunde* (Merseburger, Berlin, 1963). So when you consult a dictionary of music, do not content yourself with two or three English or American ones. Check the same subject in French, German, Italian, or Spanish publications of comparable stature; and if you know these languages, all well and good; if not, ask a friend or teacher to help. You will be surprised, even shocked at times, by the differences not only of opinion but even of fact. When you find seriously conflicting information, narrow it down and undertake, if possible, detailed research until the matter is clarified – at any rate in your own mind. You too, like the authors of articles, have the right to accept or reject information if you find it unconvincing.

Even more alarming perhaps than the conflict of different opinions and statements is the circumstance, by no means rare, whereby an apparent consensus of testimony supported by distinguished works of reference turns out to be demonstrably false. The date of Benedetto Pallavicino's death is given as 6 May 1601 in the following works – Grove (1954), Baker (1958), *Dizionario* Ricordi (1959), *Encyclopédie de la Musique* (1961), Riemann (1961), *MGG* (1962), *Enciclopedia della Musica* (1964), *La Musica – Dizionario* (1968), *Dictionnaire de la Musique* (1970), Riemann – *Ergänzungsband, Personenteil L-Z* (1975), *MGG Supplement E-Z* (1979).

The various later publications have either copied the date from earlier dictionaries or relied on an article going back to 1962, where the same date appears without any reference to a primary or secondary source. But if we look at a well-known book by Henry Prunières – *Monteverdi:*

His Life and Work (London and New York, 1926; reprinted New York, 1972) – the correct date of 26 November 1601 appears twice in the text (pp.11, 26) and again in the footnotes (p.208, n.13), where the author thanks Pietro Torelli, director of the Archivio di Stato in Mantua, and quotes the death-certificate *verbatim* as it is found in the archives. Thus a fact that was established beyond all doubt in 1926 suffered subsequent distortion and an awesome multiplicity of duplication which has undoubtedly wrought havoc along the byways of unsuspecting scholarship.

In the final resort, it is the human mind that must be brought into play whenever we need to select information, for no matter how much raw material may be placed at our disposal by a computer programmed to retrieve, let us say, all the books and articles written about J.S. Bach's instrumental music, we must learn to choose precisely what is suitable for our purpose and sound from a scientific point of view. No electronic gadgetry can properly and effectively undertake for us this final process of evaluation.

Part Two

Some Basic Materials

Three
Reference Works and Catalogues

'What maketh yow to han al this labour?'
'Ful many a cause . . .'
Chaucer: *The Friar's Tale*

Just as there are bibliographies of bibliographies, so there are reference books about reference books; and if busy musicians can afford the time to survey – at least briefly – the general landscape of second knowledge they would do well to consult *Music Reference and Research Materials* by Vincent Duckles. Originally published in London and New York in 1967, it is constantly being updated and reprinted with a view to maintaining its usefulness and excellence as a reference tool. The scope of its entries under 'Dictionaries and Encyclopedias' alone, with some 300 titles, is enough to humble any would-be researcher who might think that a quick answer to a question can easily be found.

As was made clear in the previous chapter, it is quite possible to look for information in one source only and discover an apparently plausible article, written by an acknowledged expert, that supplies exactly what is needed. But even experts can make mistakes, and they would be the first to admit that research, given its rapid rate of advance, is rarely up-to-date in a general work of reference for the simple reason that works of this nature and complexity take several years to produce, so that the resulting time-lag between writing a contribution and seeing it in print could – and usually does – exclude the intervening research.

In order not to confuse the reader by offering an embarrassment of bibliographical riches, only the most readily available works will be discussed, since outward expansion in research presents no problem once a firm foundation has been laid. That foundation may have to be repaired and strengthened as time goes on: the main point is to begin with both eyes open to the possibility of improvement. Despite their size and complexity, new reference works appear more frequently than is generally supposed.

Dictionaries and Encyclopedias

Quite apart from the multi-volume works of reference to which this section limits itself, there are numerous one-volume compilations – large and small – providing rapid retrieval, though not as detailed as can be found in the major publications.* It should also be borne in mind that excellent articles on a wide variety of musical topics can be seen in general encyclopedias such as the *Encyclopaedia Britannica* or the *New Catholic Encyclopedia*, with its special coverage of religious music and liturgy.

Grove's *Dictionary of Music and Musicians*, named after its first editor Sir George Grove, began publication just a century ago, in 1879. Then in four volumes, it contained an excellent index, rarely found in dictionaries then or since. By 1954 it had reached its fifth edition, and though much improved in many respects the standard of its articles was uneven. Some have been reprinted ever since the first edition, with hardly any change apart from the up-dating of the bibliography, yet the books whose titles were added have not always been drawn upon to renovate the research in the article itself. Other entries reflect the cut-and-paste approach, with three authors from three different generations dealing with one composer or one topic. Occasionally the cutting-out of old material to make way for new brings about a hiatus or *non sequitur*, and in other instances vital information is hard to find, since articles are not organized on a consistent basis. Nevertheless, Grove V

---

*Two reference works in the single volume category have withstood the test of time with notable success: the *Oxford Companion to Music*, by Percy A. Scholes; and the *Harvard Dictionary of Music*, by Willi Apel.

has made countless friends throughout the English-speaking world, and by the time it has been superseded by Grove VI (1980) there will be a demand for far higher standards. While it is to be hoped that libraries, if not individuals, will not be slow to replace the old by the new, the enormous cost of the new edition may deter institutions with limited budgets. If you have to use the old edition, do so with caution, and be careful to check all literature on a given topic, especially if published after 1961 (the date of the Supplementary volume).

Among the most useful of French reference works are the two-volume *Larousse de la Musique* (1957), rich in illustrations and in brief but informative articles covering biographies, title entries, and topics; the three-volume *Encyclopédie de la Musique* (1958-61) organized on somewhat unusual lines – essays on music in society precede the main section, in which slightly more space is devoted to topics than to biographies; and the more recent *Dictionnaire de la Musique* (edited by Marc Honegger) which separates composers and their works from essays on form, technique, and instruments.

In Germany pride of place must be given to *Die Musik in Geschichte und Gegenwart*, which began publication in 1949 and is – at the time of writing thirty years later – still growing thanks to the series of supplementary volumes intended both to repair omissions in the original alphabet and to correct and improve where necessary. All articles, whether biographical or technical, are carefully organized and expertly edited. Generous space is allocated to illustrations and to bibliography; complete lists of works are given for all major composers. Since these lists are 'run on' rather than printed in such a way that each new title appears on a new line, hunting for an individual piece can sometimes prove tiresome; the best solution therefore is to make use of a thematic catalogue if one exists for the composer you wish to study. In addition to the vast coverage of music in all its aspects, there are many articles on poets and librettists. Quick-reference lists of articles, authors, and illustrations appear at the end of each volume.

Less bulky and more concise, Riemann's *Musik-Lexikon* in its 12th edition is nevertheless a highly reliable and practical source of information. There are no portraits of composers in the *Personenteil* (at first two volumes, A-K and L-Z; then a supplementary volume for each), and no pictures of musical instruments in the *Sachteil* (though this volume does contain musical examples, also diagrams and facsimiles); this means that more space is given to articles and bibliographies. A useful feature of the articles on earlier composers is the listing of modern editions for scholarly or practical use. Music of different types, however, calls for different treatment: the excellent Mozart catalogue provides a synoptic view of his *oeuvre* mentioning actual titles, dates, and Köchel numbers, whereas the Lassus catalogue lists only collections. In fact one could read the entire entry on Lassus and hardly be aware of a single title of any of his compositions, which is perhaps an example of pure musicology carried too far. Nevertheless Riemann is far from being pedantic. It must be the only dictionary to contain a joke entry on a non-existent composer, in this instance Guglielmo Baldini, alias Willibald [Gurlitt], editor of this edition. Assistant editors are obviously not lacking in a sense of humour.

In Italian, the four-volume *Enciclopedia della Musica* (1963-64) is still serviceable and contains a number of well-written general articles on composers, preceding the detailed biographical and critical studies. For more up-to-date bibliography, however, it is better to consult the six-volume *La Musica* (1966-1970), of which the first four volumes ('Enciclopedia Storica') deal with 81 major composers and a good sampling of technical and historical topics, while the last two ('Dizionario') cover lesser figures and subjects omitted from the first group. The problem with this kind of division is that some readers will find their favourite composers relegated to the minority classification, and blame the editors for making arbitrary decisions. The most modern of the Italian reference works is the six-volume *Enciclopedia Rizzoli*, a luxury publication for which both Ricordi and Rizzoli are jointly responsible.

For coverage of special topics such as national music, recourse may be had to reference works in languages other than English, French, German and Italian. The two-volume Dutch *Encyclopedie van de Muziek* (1956-57) is valuable in this respect, as are also the Spanish *Diccionario de la música Labor* (1954, 2 vols.), and the more extensive Swedish dictionary, *Sohlmans Musiklexikon* (1948-52, 4 vols.). As in cases discussed above, there are many single-volume works of reference capable of launching a research project even if they cannot continue beyond a certain point, and these should therefore not be totally over-looked.

Histories of Music

Over the past two centuries, musical historiography has undergone significant changes in scope, style, and attitude, reflecting at all times the spirit of the age in which it flourished, and the personal preferences of individual authors. Far from being disadvantageous, however, these special characteristics allow us to grasp more easily the music of the 18th century as seen by Dr Burney in his *General History of Music* (4 vols., 1776-89; reprinted frequently since 1935), or the scientific approach of his contemporary Sir John Hawkins in his *General History of the Science and Practice of Music* (5 vols., 1776; also much reprinted). Since their day and age, the multi-volume history of music written by one man is a rarity – August Wilhelm Ambros did not live to complete his ambitious and thorough-going *Geschichte der Musik*, which began publication in 1887, though it was finally brought up-to-date and revised by several colleagues.

By the time of Ambros, the information dam had already burst, with the result that large-scale histories were obliged to draw upon the talents of specialists. Their role was to contribute chapters to a composite volume in a series, or an entire volume if they were equal to the task. In English, the most useful sets are the *New Oxford History of Music*, which got off to a slow start in 1954 (the earlier volumes are uneven in quality, and less reliable than recent ones) and the American series of W.W. Norton, which began in 1940 with Gustave Reese's *Music in the Middle Ages* (now in course of revision) but is still incomplete.

In French, two important undertakings stand in marked contrast one to the other. Robert Bernard's *Histoire de la Musique* (3 vols., 1961-63) is lavishly illustrated but lacks a good bibliography, while Roland-Manuel's similarly titled two-volume set has no pictorial matter, although there are musical examples and diagrams. The Italians are weak in this field, for the Corte-Pannain *Storia della Musica* in three volumes dates back to 1935, while the more recent work in two volumes by Giulio Confalonieri appeals to the general reader rather than the serious researcher. This *Storia della Musica*, rich in illustrations, came out in 1958: it contains no music examples, but its bibliographies and indices are serviceable. German scholars have placed us in their debt with the series edited (1927-31) by Ernst Bücken, entitled *Handbuch der Musikwissenschaft* but really a history of music in ten volumes by various experts; and more recently with the *Musikgeschichte in Bildern*, edited by Besseler and Schneider (from 1961) and intended to provide thorough iconographical coverage of all periods of musical history.

Catalogues and Inventories

Research, even of the most elementary kind, pre-supposes the availability and use of catalogues and inventories. A century ago, such tools were extremely rare in the world of music, and it therefore became a matter of urgent necessity to manufacture them and make them accessible to scholars, librarians, and musicians by whatever means of publication might be convenient. Robert Eitner was one of the leaders in the field of bibliography, publishing his *Bibliographie der Musiksammelwerke* in 1877 as a contribution towards the listing and location of printed music collections of the 16th and 17th centuries. Later he began a far more ambitious project – a biographical and bibliographical dictionary of source-materials from Anno Domini 1 up to the middle of the 19th century – much too large, in fact, for any one man to accomplish; but such was his industry and determination that within the term of four years, or a little more (1900-1904), he had produced the ten-volume *Quellen-Lexikon* (to give it its short title) which, imperfect though it was, helped countless scholars and encouraged them to carry on with the good work.

For musicians in search of secondary source-materials, the work of Eitner and his followers may not at first seem to be very important, since the need to discover how many modern editions exist of a certain piano solo, song, quartet or orchestral work can usually be satisfied by recourse to specialized modern handbooks listing the music literature of individual instruments, of choirs, orchestras, and the like. Much valuable information can also be gleaned from the set of catalogues published by the BBC in London, for their library of reference and performing scores is one of the largest in the world. Every type and genre of music is included, in alphabetical order of composers, and after each title may be found details of publisher, scoring, and duration.

Since many catalogues of printed music stop at the beginning of the 19th century (not because cataloguers have no affinity with music from 1800 onwards, but because the amount of published material grew to staggering proportions), research into 'recent' rather than 'early' music is best pursued in the great catalogues of the main copyright libraries – those institutions entitled by law to a free copy of each published work. Irrespective of whether the system is based on extensive card-catalogues or on the hefty, back-breaking, hernia-happy tomes favoured by the old libraries, it generally yields impressive results when used methodically and thoroughly.

If, however, musicians become interested in primary source-materials, they must be prepared to look for these in specific libraries, and to bear in mind at all times that they may be dealing with a unique manuscript or the only surviving copy of a rare printed work; and at the other end of the scale with a cornucopia of manuscripts (each containing a copy of a given work, but with differences due to the scribes responsible), or a rash of printed editions that may appear to overlap each other though in fact they usually contain important variants.

Global and national levels.

This information occurs on at least four levels: global, national, local, and specific. On the global level, the International Musicological Society and the International Association of Music Libraries have, since 1949, undertaken to replace Eitner's *Quellen-Lexikon* by an International Inventory of Musical Sources, shown as RISM on the spine of each volume after the French version of this title: *Répertoire International des Sources Musicales*. These volumes are not inexpensive, but they represent the results of countless hours of toil on the part of scholars and librarians; they sum up for us masses of correspondence and thousands of miles of travel, for it is not always possible to make detailed inventories (especially of remote libraries) with microfilm as the sole aid and prop of the cataloguer.

Each volume of RISM has its particular *mode d'emploi*, based on the kind of material included and the editorial method adopted. In most cases references are clear and straightforward, though musicians unfamiliar with the series as a whole may wish to note that the signs for location are based on internationally recognized letters used for motor-car identification: B for Belgium, CH (Confédération Helvétique) for Switzerland, D for Germany, and so on. These letters appear at the head of each national section in the lists of library sigla. In the volume dealing with Manuscripts of Polyphonic Music, 11th to early 14th century (edited by Gilbert Reaney, Munich-Duisburg, 1966), this list appears on pp.25-30, and immediately following is an alphabetical list of the same material (pp.31-35).

Let us assume that you are looking at the brief list of composers on p.823, and wish to trace a work by Eustacius Leodiensis, otherwise known as Eustace of Liège, whose name is listed in the left-hand column. After it comes the location siglum *St. Paul*, which has nothing to do with London or Minnesota. In order to trace it, turn to the alphabetical list of sigla, where on p. 35 you will see: *St. Paul* – St. Paul in Kärnten, Stiftsbibliothek, 27.2°.25. There is a cross-reference on p.29 under the heading (A): Österreich, reminding you that the order of countries followed throughout the catalogue follows not the motor-car letter but the initial of the country, so that Ö is towards the end of the volume, on p.809-10. There you will read that the manuscript in question could not be found at the time of investigation, and that the motet by Eustace is 'a wretched piece of work, an attempt to reconstruct a three-part polyphonic motet on the basis of Guido of Arezzo's method of composing by vowels'.

This should serve to remind researchers that in musicology you are obliged to deal with wretched compositions as well as masterpieces, and that a musician-musicologist such as Professor Reaney can sometimes, by virtue of a timely warning, save you an expensive journey to the south-east corner of Austria. Individual compositions can be traced with similar ease: for example *Amours dont je sui espris me fait chanter* (p.826) bears the reference *Mo* 253. On p.33 *Mo* is translated as Montpellier, Faculté de Médecine, H 196, whereupon you turn to the section for France, finding a full description and complete thematic index of the manuscript on pp.272-369. The title in question appears as No.253 (See illustration on page 30), folio 298 verso – 300 verso, and the opening phrase (incipit) for the other two voices of the motet, *L'autrier au douz mois d'avril* and the tenor, *Chose tassin*. An almost identical approach works perfectly with the volumes dealing with later medieval manuscripts, catalogued by Kurt von Fischer.

The RISM catalogues of printed music cover a much wider range, and cannot list every work in a collection, let

Some Basic Materials

251. f. 295v–297

Sal - ve, vir - go vir - gi - num, sal - ve

Est il donc ein - si que la be - le

Aptatur

252. f. 297–298v

En mai quant ro - sier sont flou - ri

L'au - tre jour par un ma - tin che - vau - cho - ie

Hé, resvelle toi

253. f. 298v–300v

A - mours dont je sui es - pris me fait chan - ter

L'au - trier au douz mois d'av - ril

Chose tassin

Plate 1

Page from RISM Catalogue showing part of the inventory (thematic index) for the Montpellier Codex, by permission of G. Henle Verlag.

alone provide thematic indices as in the medieval volumes. But they do offer, in chronological order, titles of printed works, with place, printer, date, number of volumes, size, and number of pages, together with ancillary information and library sigla. The extant material has been divided into two separate volumes, one dealing with collections (i.e. by more than one composer), the other with printed music showing the name of one composer only. For greater detail, you should turn to Eitner's *Sammelwerke*, to Vogel's catalogue of Italian secular vocal music: *Bibliothek der gedruckten weltlichen Vocalmusik Italiens aus den Jahren 1500-1700* (2 vols., Berlin, 1892; reprinted with additions by Olms, Hildesheim, 1962), to H.M. Brown's *Instrumental Music printed before 1600* (Harvard, 1965), to Claudio Sartori's *Bibliografia della musica strumentale italiana stampata in Italia fino al 1700* (2 vols., Florence, 1952, 1968) and other comparable works.

Vogel's work is mentioned here even though it has recently been replaced by a new and impressive work in three volumes: *Bibliografia della musica italiana vocale profana pubblicata dal 1500 al 1700*, Rome, 1977. The work of Vogel and Einstein has been carried forward by François Lesure and Claudio Sartori, who have identified the authors of many anonymous poems as well as adding a considerable number of new titles and collections. But since this set has been advertised at a price of over 1,000 Swiss francs, it may be some time before the less wealthy libraries can afford to purchase it. If you have to continue using Vogel, remember that it is old and somewhat unreliable for high-quality research, even though it can still be of use as a friendly reference tool. Vogel was one of the first scholars to compile and include an index of poets and dedicatees (II, 544-575), but while this has great potential for general research and programme-building, it should not be used without careful checking.

By way of an example, look at II, 557 for a reference to what would at first appear to be a member of the Gonzaga family in Mantua. It reads as follows:

Gonzaga, Ferdinando (Ferrando, Ferrante). See Baccusi 4, Bassani 1, Bernardi 4, Bertolotti 2, Caccini Or. [*recte* Caccino, Oratio], Cifra 3, Civita, Coma 2, Gagliano M. 5, Gentile, Hoste 1, Marenzio 58, Marini B. 7, Merulo Giac., Ruffulo, Turco 2.

The problem here is that although Ferrando and Ferrante are alternative spellings of Ferdinando, we are dealing with several different and distinct members of the vast Gonzaga clan, many of whom lived outside the city of Mantua! Hoste's book of madrigals is dated 1554 and must therefore be dedicated to Don Ferrante I of Guastalla (1507-1557). His grandson Ferrante II, who lived from 1563 until 1630 was in all probability the dedicatee of works by Baccusi, Caccino, Coma, and Marenzio. Ruffulo's work is dedicated to a 'Don Ferrando, Prior of Malfetta and Lord of Guastalla', who seems to have been an ecclesiastic, not a prince, and might therefore be identified with Ferdinando, a natural son of Ottavio. Matters are further complicated by the fact that there was an eminent Don Ferrante Gonzaga of Bozzolo who fought at Lepanto, and died in 1605; and another Don Ferrante (or Ferdinando) of Castelgoffredo, who died in 1586. Either could be a candidate for the dedication of the Caccino and Coma works, both published in 1585. Such questions can be resolved only after exhaustive research in archives, and collation with historical hints found in the dedicatory epistles themselves.

The works by Bernardi, Bertolotti, Cifra, Civita, Gentile, Marini, Merulo, and Turco are all definitely dedicated to Cardinal (subsequently Duke) Ferdinando Gonzaga (1587-1626), as is proved by the wording of sub-titles, title-pages and the dates of publication. The book by Bassani was written for a much later Ferdinando: he became Marquis of Medole, a small town about 35 km north-west of Mantua. As for Marco da Gagliano's book, it is clearly inscribed to a Don Ferdinando Gonzaga who was Prior of Barletta. It must be made clear at this point that we have glanced briefly at one only of the 28 Gonzaga entries, showing it to refer to several personages whose joint life-span exceeds 170 years. It should however prove that historical research, as an ancillary to musical research, ought not to be under-estimated.

To Vogel, Sartori, and other catalogues on a national level one should certainly add the British Union Catalogue of Early Music (2 vols., London, 1957) in which Dr Edith Schnapper has brought together the listings of over 100 libraries in the British Isles in so far as printed music before 1800 is concerned. Specialized works dealing with library holdings in Europe are Charles van den Borren's 'Inventaire des manuscrits de musique polyphonique qui se trouvent en Belgique', in *Acta Musicologica* V (1933), 66-71; Paule Chaillon's 'Les fonds musicaux de quelques bibliothèques de Province', in *Fontes artis musicae* II (1955), 151-163; and Åke Davidsson's *Catalogue critique et descriptif des imprimés de musique* (Uppsala, 1952), restricted to printed music of the 16th and 17th centuries in Swedish libraries (with the exception of the Royal Library of Uppsala, which has its own catalogue). In America, Otto Albrecht's *A Census of Autograph Music Manuscripts of European Composers in American Libraries* (Philadelphia, 1953) still serves as an indispensable and basic tool even though library holdings have much increased in this area over the past quarter of a century.

Local and specific levels.

A considerable number of libraries have published detailed catalogues of their own collections, but since many were compiled years ago, and certainly long before the RISM epoch, their usefulness now may be limited. Nevertheless, they often provide fuller listings than may be found in the necessarily abbreviated entries in the RISM volumes dealing with printed music. Catalogues, published and in manuscript, are referred to in the articles on 'Libraries and Collections' in Grove V (Charles Cudworth) and VI (Rita Benton); also in the article 'Musikbibliotheken und Sammlungen' in MGG Vol.9 (columns 1034-1068) by

Richard Schaal. The most thorough bibliographical description of the catalogues is to be found in Vincent Duckles: *Music Reference and Research Materials*. It should be noted that many old libraries, of which catalogues still exist, have been destroyed, dispersed, or moved elsewhere – *habent sua fata libelli*, one might say – so that the researcher will look in vain for the Biblioteca Borghese in Rome, the Werner Wolffheim Library in Berlin, the Wilhelm Heyer Collection in Cologne, or the Library of St Michael's College in Tenbury.

By good fortune, some collections have been preserved intact, such as that of Paul Hirsch, which was acquired by the British Library, or the Stecchini manuscripts purchased by the University of California in 1958. A thematic catalogue of these manuscripts of 18th century Italian instrumental music came out in 1963. Even a brief study of the field is sufficient to demonstrate that entire libraries as well as individual items can, and sometimes do, travel halfway round the world, for there is already ample material about such peregrinations. Those who wish to follow unusual trails might consider starting with the fascinating chapter on 'Lost Music' in W.G. Hiscock's *A Christ Church Miscellany* (Oxford, 1946), or with the articles about music mislaid behind the Iron Curtain – 'Music Libraries in Eastern Europe', by Dragan Plamenac (*Notes* XIX, 1961-62).

The degree of usefulness to which a catalogue can be assigned depends to a considerable extent upon its organization and indices. Occasionally a catalogue of some magnitude, compiled by one man, proves to be useful in ways far beyond the normal scope of such a work by reason of its thorough index system. The three-volume *Catalogue of Manuscript Music in the British Museum*, by Augustus Hughes-Hughes, dates from 1906-1909 and can no longer claim to be up-to-date, yet the indices of initial words and titles enable the researcher to tap immediately the vast resources of the manuscript collection as it stood at the turn of the present century. These incipits occupy 118 pages of Vol.1 (Sacred Vocal Music), 258 pages of Vol.2 (Secular

Vocal Music), and 55 pages of Volume 3 (Instrumental Music, Treatises, Histories, Biographies, Iconography and other topics).

Few music catalogues feature extensive lists of incipits such as these, and equally rare are the exhaustive name-and-subject indices that also form a substantial part of each volume. Research into music written for historical figures in England, France, Poland, Russia, Scotland, and so forth, is made less toilsome by the convenient groupings of occasional music under those headings, most of which will repay cursory study by concrete and memorable allusions. The lengthy list for England is rich in references to its sovereigns from Richard III to Queen Victoria, but does not exclude other characters and events, as can be gathered from the faintly bizarre entries in Vol.2 (p.932): 'Glee on the death of the Duke of Cumberland, 1756', and 'Song on the O[ld] P[rices] Riots, 1809'. Among the sub-headings for Italian music in the same volume are cross-references to dialect songs from Sicily, Venice, and Naples. Cities and towns whose particular music is mentioned include Cremona, Durham, London, Modena, Namur, and Pozzuoli, where the Capuchin monks apparently inspired Pergolesi to write a scherzo-duet in Latin. The curious will also find references to songs on paintings by Titian, on the departure from Pisa of a virtuoso violoncellist, on the Royal Humane Society, and on the Duke of Wellington. Entries of a like nature in the other two volumes will also serve to amplify the necessarily general articles on people and places in less specialized publications. (See Plate 2, p.37).

On the specific level, for the student seeking to grasp the significance of a manuscript as a whole, nothing is more useful than a well-prepared inventory. These are more commonly associated with manuscripts owing to their personal and unique nature, for although a printed book may also rank as a valuable and irreplaceable *unicum*, a volume copied by hand exerts a greater fascination upon scholars and bibliophiles. Musicologists have been making inventories of manuscripts for well over a century, even though the results may not always have reached the stage of publication. Notwithstanding the modern inventory of 15th-century polyphony in Modena, Biblioteca Estense, Ms.α.X.1.11 (lat.471) – to be mentioned below – it should be noted that the librettist, lawyer, and librarian William Barclay Squire made a partial index of that source in 1892, presenting it to the British Library (then British Museum) in 1900, where it is catalogued as Additional Ms. 36490.

The main point of an inventory is to enable the reader to see at a glance the entire contents of a manuscript, in the order in which the pieces appear. This may or may not correspond with the order in which they were composed or written down, but it does impart a certain knowledge of the way in which the manuscript was compiled, and of the relationship between the repertoire and its composers. Most modern inventories provide accurate details of old and new foliation, the form of each piece, number of vocal or instrumental parts, dates and historical references, and concordances (copies of individual works in other sources). The list is usually preceded by a detailed essay on the history of the manuscript, its former owners, place of compilation, relationship with contemporaneous sources, and other matters of interest. In some cases it may be followed by transcriptions of music chosen for some remarkable feature or other, or for its historical interest.

Although inventories sometimes appear in books, they are found more frequently in periodicals whose regular and widespread distribution throughout the scholarly world assures their compilers of immediate attention. Some periodicals feature inventories occasionally, while others make a speciality of them. Over the past three decades, we have had such classics as the inventory of the Vallicelliana partbooks by Edward E. Lowinsky – *Journal of the American Musicological Society* III (1950), 173-232; of the

Plate 2

Page from the British Museum Catalogue of Manuscript Music, II, 931, showing the entries under 'England, Sovereigns of', and a reference to Elephants on stage in 1752.

36

Some Basic Materials

French Chansonnier in the Biblioteca Colombina by Dragan Plamenac – *The Musical Quarterly* XXXVII (1951), 501-542, XXXVIII (1952), 85-117 and 245-277; of the Eton Manuscript by Frank Harrison, La Clayette by Albi Rosenthal, and Paris B.N. Rés. Vm⁷ 676 by Nanie Bridgman – all in *Annales Musicologiques* I (1953); of Rome, Vatican City, San Pietro B 80 by Charles Hamm – *Revue Belge de Musicologie* XIV (1960), 40-55; of Paris, B.N. Rés. Vma 851 by Oscar Mischiati – *Rivista Italiana di Musicologia* X (1975), 265-328.

The periodical that surpasses all others in the publication of inventories is *Musica Disciplina*, whose editor Armen Carapetyan introduced this feature into the very first volume, which was then called *Journal of Renaissance and Baroque Music*. Since the good work still continues, it may not be inappropriate to list the principal contributions since 1946-47:

Aosta, Seminario: Ms without signature	II (1948), 231-257
Bologna, Biblioteca Universitaria, Ms 2216	VI (1952), 39-66
Bologna, Civico Museo Bibliografico	XX (1966), 57-94
Musicale, Ms Q16	XXIII (1969), 81-104
Bologna, Civico Museo Bibliografico	
Musicale, Ms Q15	II (1948), 231-257
Chantilly, Musée Condé, Ms 1047	VIII (1954), 59-113
	X (1956), 55-59
Dresden, Sächsische Landesbibliothek,	
Ms 1/D/506	XXVIII (1974), 81-128
Durham, Cathedral Library, Ms C.1.20	XXI (1967), 67-86
Edinburgh, National Library, Adv.Ms 5.1.15	XIII (1959), 41-80
London, British Museum, Add. Ms 29987	XII (1958), 67-104
London, British Museum, Add. Ms 57590	
(Old Hall Ms)	XXI (1967), 97-148
Lucca, Archivio di Stato, Ms fragments	I (1946), 173-191
Madrid, El Escorial, Ms IV.α.24	XXIII (1969), 41-80
Modena, Biblioteca Estense, α.M.5.24	
(lat.568)	XXIV (1970), 17-68
Modena, Biblioteca Estense, α.X.1.11	
(lat.471)	XXVI (1972), 101-144
New York, Public Library, Drexel Ms 4041	XVIII (1964), 151-202
New York, Public Library, Drexel Ms 4175	XVI (1962), 73-92

Oxford, Bodleian Library,
    Canonici Misc. 213   IX (1955), 73-104
Oxford, Christ Church Library, Mss 979-983 XXV (1971), 179-198
Paris, Bibliothèque Nationale, n.a.f. 6771   XI (1957), 38-78*
                                     XVII (1963), 57-78
Paris, Bibliothèque Nationale,
    fonds italien 568   XIV (1960), 33-63
Paris, Bibliothèque Nationale, Rés. 2489   XXIII (1969), 117-140
Vienna, National Library, Ms. 1783   XXIII (1969), 105-116

Thematic catalogues.

It goes without saying that any *catalogue raisonné* of a particular composer's work will benefit by the inclusion of musical examples consisting of the first few notes or measures of each work, or each section of a work. The visual identification of a theme, apart from its intrinsic value, enables the reader to distinguish it from themes that may be closely related to the point of causing confusion. Although it is possible to reduce such examples to a system of letters or figures, not unlike certain kinds of tablature, the 'genuinely musical' kind of thematic index affords the reader greater ease of reference. The virtue of the let-ter—figure system is that in certain circumstances trans-posed versions of one and the same composition can be brought together and identified, as Nanie Bridgman demonstrated in her remarkable article 'L'établissement d'un catalogue par incipit musicaux', in *Musica Disciplina* IV (1950), 65-68. By extension of this system, it is possible to trace a theme whose title may be unknown, simply by changing the notes into a letter- or figure-code and then checking the formula against a specially-prepared list.

When one considers the almost imponderable bulk of extant plainchant melodies, and the frequent similarities of their initial motives, some numerical system of classifica-tion would seem to be highly desirable. It has in fact been accomplished, in a remarkable two-volume *Index of Gregorian Chant* (Cambridge, Mass., 1969) by John E. Bryden and David G. Hughes. Tens of thousands of incipits drawn

*See Plate 3, p.40.

39

No.	Folio	Beginning of Text	Voices	Form	Composer	Concordances	Remarks
108	54	Cortois et sages	3^1	B	(Egidius)	Mod, no. 68	Acrostic Clemens VII. Comp. about 1378. Edn. ApF, no. 57 (Mod).
109	54v/55	Quant Theseus, Hercules et Jason (C 1) Ne quier veoir (C 2)	4^{1+1}	B	(Machaut)	Mach; Ch, no. 88	Edn. LuMa I, B 34; SchraMa, 124.
110	55	Bonte de corps en armes	3^1	B	—	Str, no. 121 (3^9)	Acrostic Bertrand [du Gueselin] († 1380). In Str with Contrafactum Text Beata es Virgo. Edn. ApF, no. 65.
111	55v	Tres douche plasant bergiere (C 1) Reconforte toy Robin (C 2)	3^{1+1}	V	—	—	
112	56	Phiton, Phiton, beste tres veneneuse	3^1	B	(Mag. Franciscus)	Ch, no. 18	Gaston Phébus, Count of Foix. Edn. ReaCh, 98. Facs. MGG, IV, pl. 28 (Ch); Gen, pl. 10 (Ch).
113	56v	Dame qui fust si tres bien assene	3^1	B	—	—	Strongly related to Machaus B 23 (cf. LuMa II, 25*). Edn. LuMa I, B 23a (p. 26, Fragm. only).
114	56v/57	En wyflyc beildt ghestadt van sinne	3^1	B	—	—	Edn. LenN, no. 1 of the music section.
115	57	Contre le temps et la sason (C) He, mari, mari, vous soiiez onni (T)	3^{1+1}	V	—	—	Isorhythmic Tenor.

Plate 3

Page from *Musica Disciplina*, XI, 65, showing part of Professor Kurt von Fischer's inventory of the Reina Codex, Paris, B.N., n.a.f. 6771.

from graduals, antiphoners, processionals and other liturgical books have been placed in accessible order – by title in
vol. 1, and by number in vol.2 – so that one type of information can be immediately related to the other.

Thematic catalogues of works by individual composers
are now so numerous that they have themselves become
the subject of lists and catalogues. In 1954 the New York
Public Library reprinted from its own *Bulletin* a modest but
useful *Check-List of Thematic Catalogues*, while more
recently Barry Brook brought forth his ambitious *Thematic
Catalogues in Music* (New York, 1972). As in the sister
realms of general cataloguing, certain classics rightly rank
as bibliographical triumphs: J.S. Bach by Wolfgang
Schmieder, Beethoven by Georg Kinsky, Haydn by
Anthony van Hoboken, Mozart by Ludwig Köchel,
Richard Strauss by E.H. Müller von Asow. As for Vivaldi,
his music has tempted several industrious cataloguers, including Mario Rinaldi (1945), Marc Pincherle (1948),
Antonio Fanna (1968), Peter Ryom (1973), with the result
that concordances to the different systems have been compiled and published with a view to making life either more
or less complicated for the researcher, depending on when
and where an enquiry is made. It may soon be time to put
the red-headed priest into a computer.

Useful if out-dated thematic catalogues are occasionally
associated with large-scale publications such as collected
works or historical monuments of music. The series of
volumes containing transcriptions from the seven choir-
books at Trent begins with such an index (*Denkmaler der
Tonkunst in Österreich*, VII), while the old Breitkopf
editions of Bach and Palestrina feature generously illustrated lists of works in vols.XLVI and XXXIII respectively. Library catalogues rarely blossom with themes, but
when they do there is much to be studied, as in G.E.P.
Arkwright's *Catalogue of Music in the Library of Christ
Church, Oxford* (Part II) which prints 180 pages of themes
from manuscripts of vocal music by unknown authors. The
RISM volumes devoted to early manuscripts offer a com-

parable service over a much wider range of repertoire.

As an example of a thematic index and its parergon, Franklin Zimmerman's two volumes on Henry Purcell demonstrate the modern approach at its most efficient. The *Analytical Catalogue* (London, 1963) presents an overview of the composer's works arranged in a logical and numerical sequence, which is cross-indexed scientifically in a smaller volume – *Melodic and Intervallic Indexes* (Philadelphia, 1975). The main volume divides Purcell's music into four distinct categories: Sacred Vocal, Secular Vocal, Dramatic, and Instrumental Music, with a handful of didactic examples as a coda. Suitably sub-divided, these sections provide incipits for every single piece, even down to the individual movements in an anthem or opera. Each work has a number, while the movements are set off by smaller-size numbers accompanied by a,b,c, for sub-sections.

Turn to page 18, and you find No.19, 'I was glad when they said unto me'. Just below the title, the reference (XIV, 97) gives the volume and page number of the Purcell Society Edition, and this is followed by the date (*ca.*1683-4), along with the Biblical source of the text. Vocal and instrumental scoring is shown by abbreviations which are in standard use, though if there is any doubt they are explained on pp. xvii and xviii at the beginning of the catalogue. After the musical incipits comes a list of manuscripts transmitting this particular anthem. Note that the numbers in heavy type refer to autographs or part-autographs: the key to these references can be found on pp.442-481. Under 'Editions' the Purcell Society details are given once again, followed by the years of printed editions prior to 1850. These may be checked against fuller references on pp.482-528 (Appendix IV and its Addenda). No list of modern editions appears, and while this may be a matter for regret, it must be borne in mind that a full account of such information would have increased the size (and cost) of the catalogue considerably. There is, however, a very useful section headed 'Commentary' providing

historical and bibliographical data beyond what has gone
before. Special books or articles are noted under the final
heading 'Literature', and it should be further noted that
general information on each genre is provided at the end of
each section – Anthems (p.69), Services (p.110), Catches
(p.129), Odes and Birthday Songs (p.177), Songs (p.232),
Incidental Music (p.292), Operas and Semi-Operas
(p.343), Keyboard (p.368), String Fantasias (p.382),
Sonatas (p.398). A more detailed bibliography may be
seen in the same author's *Henry Purcell: His Life and
Times* (London, 1967).

The small volume of indices (1975) will prove useful to
those having a theme in mind but no rapid means of iden-
tifying it. While the Foreword is helpful for the initiated,
some further assistance may not come amiss if perhaps you
have never used this type of catalogue before. First, write
down the theme as accurately as you can remember it,
transposing to C major or C minor, no matter what key you
think it may be in. Next, write the letter-names, using a
zero(0) for each rest or group of rests. If the same pitch
occurs twice or more in succession, write down the letter
once only, as in the example below:

Ex. 1

G 0 G F 0 F Eb 0 Eb D

If however a pitch is repeated after a rest, the letter should
also be repeated. This principle also applies to a note
followed by the same note an octave above or below.
Having fortified yourself with the list of symbols, G 0 G F 0
F E♭ 0 E ♭ D, turn to the Pitch Index (pp.1-65) and start to
check your letters against those beginning in column 4
(immediately below the 'M' of Melodic index). They start
with C, gradually moving up the scale: each successive
column follows the same rule. You will find the themes
beginning with G 0 G on pp.42-43, where a short search

will reveal the wanted theme:

B 2 44 e G 0 G F 0 F E♭ 0 E♭ D 328/8A2 08,052

which being translated means: beginning pitch B at the second octave (see Table III, p.viii), time-signature 4/4, key E minor, theme, Catalogue No.328, sub-section 8a, second entry, Purcell Society vol.VIII p.52. The second index (intervallic) performs the same task in a slightly different way. Each catalogue has its particular *modus operandi*, which may require ten or fifteen minutes of study if you really want to master it: this time is never wasted.

On using a library

It is a sad fact that materials in libraries of a modest or functional nature frequently suffer from the depredations of students who have little or no respect for books and music. Pages are torn out, margins become the unwilling receptacles of unpalatable glosses, passages are underlined in all colours of the rainbow. Books 'disappear' and music 'vanishes'. Although it may seem superfluous to point out that a strict code of conduct is not only recommended but enforced in the great public and private libraries of the world, it is not uncommon to see ball-point pens at work in the close proximity of precious manuscripts, or pages of an incunabulum being carelessly or roughly turned in a helter-skelter hunt for dissertation fodder. Care must always be taken to follow the rules of conduct laid down by individual institutions, and above all to treat materials with the greatest caution and respect. The best general guide to libraries is a series begun in 1967 by Rita Benton: a *Directory of Music Research Libraries* forming a multi-volume reference work of extreme usefulness and importance. Each entry gives all the information necessary to the researcher concerned with the problems of making initial contact and gaining access to a collection.

Four
Musical Literature

> And grant that a man read all ye books of
> musick that ever were wrote, I shall not
> allow that musick is or can be understood
> out of them, no more than the tast of
> meats out of cookish receipt books.
>
> Roger North: *The Musicall Gramarian*

Although books about music range over an amazing variety of topics, those most likely to be of service to the
practical musician – aside from the dictionaries and histories already discussed – are biographical and analytical
studies, investigations of a particular type of music, and
historical or technical studies of individual instruments.
Every kind of knowledge contributes to mature and memorable artistry. Instinct can carry one so far only: the post-
prodigy, remaining fully equipped from a technical point of
view, can grow only in mental stature. The best way of
assuring that this will happen is to read regularly and
selectively in those areas of musical knowledge that seem
most helpful and appropriate. Since there is no stemming
the flow of information and ideas, the best solution is to
immerse oneself in it as far as circumstances permit.

Analytical and Biographical

In the introduction to his thoughtful and stimulating study,
Music and Painting (London, 1973), Edward Lockspeiser
made the point that present-day musical history 'is largely
based on the idea of technical analysis. This is not surprising since we live in a technological age. The humanistic

approach seems to be overshadowed'. Many who read, either for business or pleasure, the vast and ever-growing literature about music will surely agree, for it is incomparably easier to write plausible analysis than to give the impression that musical criticism should belong to the sphere of humane letters. Not that there is anything wrong with technology or analysis. It is simply that they are best regarded as a means to an artistic end, and relegated to tables at the back of a volume instead of embarrassing the language and trying the patience of the reader.

These technical and humanistic elements need not, however, be mutually exclusive. Everything depends upon the genius (or lack of it) in a given author. Sir Donald Tovey, a classical scholar as well as a consummate musician, produced a series of essays, still admirable, whose major virtue lies in their ability to hold the reader's attention, whether or not he fully understands the technicalities of the topic. Those *Essays in Musical Analysis* (6 vols., London, 1935-39) have recently demonstrated their intrinsic worth in a reprint, which the younger generation should get to know as soon as possible. Alec Robertson, who lived in Rome for many years, wrote an illuminating book – *The Interpretation of Plainchant* (London, 1937) – with a purely practical end in view, yet he succeeded in bringing clarity, warmth, and understanding to a subject which many must have found forbidding in prior treatises.

To the insight and sensitivity of such men should be contrasted the often mechanical, plodding, and ultimately uninspiring 'textbook analysis' of masterpieces whose very soul, shattered into a thousand fragments, thereby destroys the mischief wrought by its destroyer, yet at the same time brings disillusionment to a student rash enough to think that since music – like a clock – measures out time it can be taken apart piece by piece until its secret is finally revealed.

If it be thought that such an approach is foreign to our own times, belonging rather to a barbarous and better-forgotten past, let us glance at this cadence from Purcell's *Fly, bold rebellion*, a welcome song for Charles II (1683), found in vol. 15 of the Purcell Society Edition:

Ex. 2

Here is a typical textbook analysis:

> The cadential formula subdominant-dominant-tonic
> is used in the bass, and one expects the progressions
> $IV - I_4^6 - V - I$. The IV becomes as IV_9 by the introduc-
> tion of passing-tones. It is followed not by I_4^6 but by I_4^6
> with the tone d as a *seconde ajoutée* which makes the
> chord a VI_2. Then the d is taken to e flat. As soon as
> this e flat occurs, the chord becomes a 'pseudo sec-
> ondary dominant', a chord which appears more or less
> accidentally and gives added colour (here the Mixo-
> lydian mode). As it is no regular functional secondary
> dominant, it is not resolved to a B flat triad but is
> followed by the regular V_7 in F major, whereby the e
> flat is taken downwards to c, and the e natural is
> introduced as a cross-relation.*

Men of letters, both eminent and average, have often
been known to wonder whether the business of writing
about music should be considered a secret art or a pseudo-
science. That it sometimes tends to embody the less admirable features of both was demonstrated by George Bernard Shaw's devastatingly accurate parody of musical
analysis in *Music in London*, Vol. 2 when applied to Hamlet's soliloquy on suicide:

> Shakespear, dispensing with the customary exordium,
> announces his subject at once in the infinitive, in

*D. Schelderup-Ebbe: *Purcell's Cadences* (Oslo University Press, 1962).

which mood it is presently repeated after a short connecting passage in which, brief as it is, we recognize the alternative and negative forms on which so much of the significance of repetition depends. Here we reach a colon; and a pointed pository phrase, in which the accent falls decisively on the relative pronoun, brings us to the first stop.

It is perfectly possible and indeed allowable to analyse 'To be, or not to be . . .' in this fashion, though whether it adds very much to the stature of either Hamlet or Shakespear is dubious in the extreme. Similarly, much of the same kind of musical analysis can either be done by a moderately capable first-year student of form or harmony (done, but preferably not published); or if the aim and object is entirely mistaken – as often happens – it should never be done at all.

When the topic is carried on from analysis to function, comparable objections may be raised; but even though they have been raised, it is by no means certain that the message has reached the many. As Kaikhosru Shapurji Sorabji has so wisely stated:

> All that infantilistic babble about 'form', 'subjects', 'development' and all the rest of the classroom claptrap, tells us less than nothing about the music: no more than a metatarsal of an inhabitant of Mohenjo-Daro tells us what the man said, felt, thought or did. If it did, and it were possible to verify, we should be in the realm not of archaeology but psychometry. It is high time to declare roundly that all that pseudo-anatomical nonsense of the text-books and the analytical programme is so much pernicious and noxious rubbish, confusing the issues and darkening counsel. It distracts attention from what matters – the music – to subordinate and subsidiary matters that, in the totality of the music, are as germane thereto as a man's skeleton to the whole of him.

Some of the most persuasive among literary historians of music began their careers as art historians. Charles van den Borren made the change as a young man, but the discipline learnt in his studies of the visual arts stood him in good stead when it came to the difficult matter of writing about music, and in consequence one can still read his *Guillaume Dufay* (Brussels, 1925) with pleasure even though the research must be updated. Nino Pirrotta, another former art historian, demonstrates his continuing concern for a newer and better interpretation of musico-theatrical history in *Li due Orfei* (Turin, 1969), in which he is ably seconded by an expert in stage design, Elena Povoledo. Although men of letters who turn to music are less numerous than one might hope for, the handful of great names exerts a powerful and perpetual attraction. If Romain Rolland's study *Beethoven the Creator* (London, 1929) is still his most widely read musical work, his earlier *Histoire de l'Opéra en Europe avant Lulli et Scarlatti* remains a classic of enormous value.

Then there are the professional historians. Their view of culture and history, as deep as it is broad, sustains the natural development of a critical biography in a way that mere analysis (psycho or musical) could never hope to match. Yet there are many admirers of C.S. Terry's *Bach – a Biography* (London, 1928) who have to be reminded that the author was a professor of history, not of music. Another classic of musicological literature, F.T. Arnold's *The Art of Accompaniment from a Thorough-Bass* (London, 1931), speaks eloquently for the erudition of a man whose university appointment was not in music, but in German language and literature. In more recent years, Jacques Barzun's inspiring work on Berlioz and his contemporaries encouraged a world-wide revival of interest in nineteenth-century French music.

Two excellent biographies of composers were written by men who rank neither as musicologists nor as historians. Sacheverell Sitwell's *Liszt* (London, 1934) reflects the multi-faceted and bizarre brilliance of an age of virtuosi that was totally different from ours even though we are plentifully supplied with musical acrobats. It was the personality that mattered, not the acrobatics, and Sitwell emphasizes this with a superb sense of style. Sir Thomas Beecham's study of *Frederick Delius* (London, 1959), the natural outcome of a lifetime's advocacy of the music, resembles the Liszt book in its total omission of musical examples and technical analysis. Yet the spirit of Delius's music is somehow conveyed to the reader in an evaluation at once sympathetic and critical, which is not surprising when we recall Beecham's thoughts on criticism. Writing of the cool reception given to *Appalachia*, he says:

> Fortunately it is not those who write about music whose opinions ultimately influence its destinies, and one of the anachronisms of our age is the belief, on the part of old-fashioned editors, that it is still necessary to include among their regular staff men who know very little about the fundamentals of music, who cannot distinguish the merits of one work from another, and who rarely lose the chance of mistaking talent for genius and vice-versa.

It is wrong to believe that a biography can be enjoyed only if you happen to like the composer's music. Very little of Ferrucio Busoni's music is performed or recorded today, yet E.J. Dent's biography of this remarkable and fascinating figure (Oxford, 1933, recently reprinted) qualifies as a literary masterpiece in its own right. Dent's knowledge of European languages, his lively style, his friendship with the composer, and his penetrating glances at the music of the late 19th and early 20th centuries – all combine to make this biography not only instructive but eminently readable. The illustrations, list of works, details of Busoni's repertoire as pianist and conductor, together with the excellent index add greatly to the value of the book, which fellow-virtuosi will appreciate if only for the composer's satirical poem *Virtuosenlaufbahn*, brilliantly translated (p. 107) by Dent into rhyming English quatrains.

With three or four notable exceptions, composers who lived before the age of Bach and Handel have yet to enjoy the high standard of biographical and critical research that is normally observed in works dealing with composers of the 18th century and later. Glenn Watkins on *Gesualdo* (London, 1973), E.H. Fellowes on *William Byrd* (London, 1948), Carol MacClintock on *Giaches de Wert* (Rome, 1966) and Ralph Kirkpatrick on *Domenico Scarlatti* (Princeton, 1953) are all classics, but there are no comparable studies – at the time of writing – on Josquin, Lassus, Andrea Gabrieli, Monteverdi, Cavalli, Schütz and Charpentier, to name but a handful of luminaries.

H.J. Moser's book on the life and music of *Heinrich Schütz* (Kassel, 1936, revised 1954) achieved sufficient renown to qualify for a translation into English by Carl Pfatteicher (St Louis, 1959), but once again the casual reader, unable to devote weeks to the study of a 700-page tome, and deprived of an index of incipits, faces constant frustration. Regrettably, the able translator did not live to see his work in print, and those who saw it through the press allowed numerous misprints to pass uncorrected. Although some of these are obvious enough to be checked without too much trouble, others have been known to cause mystification. What, for instance, is the meaning of 'the primitive Turin *mentre vaga angioletta* form' (p.466)? The tyro might be excused for wondering what Guarini's poem was doing in a city in the north-western part of Italy, and why it should rank as a primitive form. The true explanation is that we are dealing with the composer Turini, not the city (Torino); moreover it is Francesco (not Gregorio as in the confused index of names), and the work in question is found in his book of madrigals for three voices, two violins, and basso continuo (Venice, 1629).

Books derived from doctoral dissertations not infrequently pose awkward problems for the innocent reader, who may be unaware of the fact that academic requirements – as interpreted by the more platitudinous of our pedants – force writers who may possess at least the rudiments of talent and style to abandon not only these but also the notion of logical synthesis. Instead of placing like with like, enabling their audience to grasp a work as a whole, these writers dissect and destroy by discussing only one small portion of it, artificially linked with various other *disjecta membra* from similar works. A study of *Francesco Cavalli* by Jane Glover (London, 1978) never discusses an opera as a whole. The operas are divided and sub-divided into such categories as Sources, Method of Composition, Aria, Recitative, Chorus, and so forth, which means that the reader who is about to hear or attend a performance of *Giasone* must content himself with a dozen references in the index leading him to a dozen pieces of a jigsaw puzzle hopelessly short of completion. Further confusion results from the student ploy of 'padding' a bibliography, for much vital information contained in listed books and articles is mysteriously lacking in the book itself.

A similar technique is put to work in *English Court Odes: 1660-1820*, by Rosamund McGuiness (Oxford, 1971), where a basically fascinating topic is subjected to an unrelenting process of fragmentation, so that in more than 200 pages only two descriptions of complete odes can be found. Moreover, one of them can be traced only with notable difficulty, since its very title is withheld on the page where the principal reference occurs ('All things their certain periods have', p.80). All those remarkable odes of Blow and Purcell are scattered to the four winds of analysis and vivisection: solos, choruses, ensembles, vocal numbers, instrumental movements, and whatnot. It is as if one had looked for an account of the history and architecture of Westminster Abbey, only to find a column of figures confirming the relative amounts of stone, wood, glass, and lead in that noble edifice.

In the medieval field, which is challenging enough without the presence of unnecessary complications, the splitting asunder of interlocking materials can sometimes lead to near-disaster. When deliberate fragmentation is applied to an already problematic and dispersed collection of source-materials such as the Worcester Fragments, only one solution is possible. Luther Dittmer's *catalogue raisonné* and transcription of these manuscripts (Rome, 1957; American Institute of Musicology) certainly contains much that is valuable, but its usefulness is sharply reduced by the way in which this material is arbitrarily divided into two sections, corresponding to the fragments in Oxford and those in Worcester. The first part of the catalogue begins on p. 12, where it is introduced by a very small figure 1. The second half, with its equally diminutive figure 2, does not begin until p. 49. The various sections appear thus:

	Oxford		*Worcester*	
Notes on Sources		15		49
The Compositions	(1-77)	17	(78-109)	50
Form and Source of Pes	(1-77)	28	(78-109)	55
Concordances	(1-77)	30	(78-109)	56
Voice-Exchange	(1-77)	33	(78-109)	57
Notes	(1-77)	35	(78-109)	58

The only practical way to deal with this information, and to avoid thumbing one's way back and forth between Oxford and Worcester, is to buy two copies of the volume, cut them up, and paste them in a master-notebook with its pages numbered 1-109, each page being reserved for all the information relating to one item only.

Letters of Composers

No matter how eloquent and persuasive a commentator may seem when we read this or that book on a composer's life and times, there is a far more direct and personal contact through the composer's own correspondence – if it survives – or, failing that, through his prefaces and other writings, such as may be found in the collection translated and edited by Oliver Strunk: *Source Readings in Music History* (New York, 1950). This, by the way, deserves to be read and absorbed as much by musicians as by scholars, for the bulk of the information stems from original sources and cannot therefore become out-of-date. Anthologies of letters offer a good introduction to the genre as a whole, and the reader who is anxious to make a start in this way would be well advised to look for such compilations as *Letters of Composers*, edited by Gertrude Norman and Miriam Lubell Schrifte (New York, 1946); *Composers on Music*, edited by Sam Morgenstern (New York, 1956; London, 1958); *Letters of Composers Through Six Centuries*, edited by Piero Weiss (Philadelphia and London, 1967). The numerous volumes devoted to letters by one composer range over vast fields of history and language, bringing in such names as Lassus, Monteverdi, Schütz, Mozart, Haydn, Beethoven, Berlioz, Mendelssohn, Liszt, Wagner, Brahms, Verdi, Richard Strauss, and Elgar.

If, as an interpreter, you have plans to concentrate for a while on the music of a certain composer, try to read a good biography and then supplement it, if possible, with a selection of his letters. Not only will they provide you with an overall impression of the kind of life he lived – they will also afford precious glimpses of his personality and his attitude towards music. This is certainly true of Beethoven's letters, collected and translated by Emily Anderson in a three-volume set published in 1961. Yet what do musicians in general know about Beethoven as a letter-writer? They know some of his music, but apart from the Heiligenstadt Testament (which has often been reprinted) the literary side of him is a largely unfamiliar one. Yet he is far from being a dull writer: much of his prose bears the same imprint as his music – forthright, intense, poetic, shot through with crazy humour and outrageous puns. There is little of the egoism we find in Wagner's letters, nothing of the dramatic flamboyance so often discovered in Berlioz. On the other hand Beethoven, for all the extemporaneous nature of his correspondence, lacks the sheer spontaneity of Mozart; and fascinating as some of the purely musical letters are, they cannot approach the classical interchange of ideas that we associate with Brahms and Joachim, or Strauss and Hofmannsthal.

The number and variety of persons to whom Beethoven addressed letters is amazing: fellow-composers, publishers, pianists, violinists, princes and potentates, relatives and friends, women whose love and affection he ardently desired, fishmongers whose pike and carp he coveted for his luncheon-table. The letters cover forty years of his life, from his 17th year onwards; and since there are nearly 1,600 of them, that makes an average of 40 a year – less than one a week. Undoubtedly many letters have been lost, either through negligence or accident, but a sufficient number remains to give us a lively impression of the composer in many different moods and engrossed in the pursuit of the most diverse topics.

From the purely musical angle, Beethoven's letters are of immense significance. They prove his deep concern at all times about artistic ideas and accuracy of publications. When a Parisian friend tells him of an attempt to arrange the Piano Sonata in A, Op. 101, for chamber ensemble, Beethoven is at first horrified. Such a step would be tantamount to transforming a miniature into a fresco painting. But good nature gets the better of him, and he agrees to look through the manuscript to see if something can be done. With careless engravers and publishers he is far less tolerant, and many of his letters are crammed full of corrections written out on roughly drawn staves. We learn much about his reliance on copyists, and we share his explosive exasperation when bars are left out and instrumental parts put into the wrong clef. His views on musical instruments, especially pianos, are made all the more fascinating by the fact that his day and age saw constant experiments and improvements, both in action and in tonal quality. One new-fangled invention, mentioned countless times and with violently varying degrees of enthusiasm, was Maelzel's metronome. Many a tempo that seemed right in Beethoven's room would prove impossible in the concert-hall.

Of some musical interest are the many canons which Beethoven was apt to jot down at the end of a hasty note to a friend. A canon, taking up relatively little space, can be easily fitted into a letter – otherwise too minute a medium for a song or even a brief instrumental piece. There is a splendid canon for the plump violinist Schuppanzigh, and half-a-dozen others for such friends as Tobias Haslinger and Friedrich Kuhlau. They and the light-hearted letters to Zmeskall von Domanovetz provide the comic relief in the tragedy that was Beethoven's life – a life which these letters illuminate so vividly.

In addition to throwing much light on musical and sociological matters, correspondence between creative artists can often intensify our understanding of a collaborative effort when, for instance, the countless fine details of an operatic work are discussed. The excellent translation by Hanns Hammelmann and Ewald Osers of the *Correspondence between Richard Strauss and Hugo von Hofmannsthal* (London, 1961) is a case in point, for in its earliest stage, the relationship between composer and librettist bore scarcely a hint of the greatness of their future collaboration. Indeed, their exchange of letters in 1900 concerning the possibility of a ballet seems almost abortive. Nothing further happened for six years as far as the correspondence reveals: then in 1906 *Elektra* appears on the scene and receives the fullest share of the limelight until 1908, when (with an almost invisible change of setting) *Der Rosenkavalier* takes its place. From then onwards, a glorious succession of artistically triumphant collaborations, including *Ariadne auf Naxos, Die Frau ohne Schatten, Die Ägyptische Helena*, and *Arabella*. Never before in the history of opera was there such a long and fruitful linking together of poet and composer, never before such a thoroughly documented account of the way in which each member of the duo perfected his own art while at the same time learning from his partner.

Yet they were, temperamentally speaking, two strangely different men. Strauss, the prodigious worker, who claimed that fine orchestration demanded the coolest and clearest of heads, a head that was not unskilled in business matters, practical and sensible in this and almost every other way; Hofmannsthal, hypersensitive and withdrawn, given to writing lengthy letters in often poetical prose, creating nevertheless in great difficulty because of a restless spirit and an inherited dislike of low atmospheric pressure and thundery weather. The marriage of these opposing temperaments ran a mainly smooth course, however, and if Strauss often made what may now seem to be outrageous demands on his librettist, cutting and adding at will, Hofmannsthal was not the kind of writer to take things lying down when he knew that some artistic principle was at stake. Although no musician himself, he knew the classical and romantic repertoire well enough to be a keen judge of the probable success – or failure – of some of Strauss's impulsive ideas.

A passage in one of Hofmannsthal's letters of 1911 demonstrates his belief that the creative aspect of music continues in and through the performance (in this case of *Ariadne*): 'It needs a real man at the conductor's desk whose heart and soul is in it – not that appalling atmosphere of the commonplace, the drab routine, the conductor with the cold heart, the opera singers who get through their music somehow'. He admired the composer as a conductor, and went not only to operas but concerts as well, for Strauss appeared frequently as a symphonic conductor during the winter seasons, reserving the summers for composition. Strauss observes with half-detached amusement the success of *Der Rosenkavalier* in Berlin and the sudden change in the attitude of von Hülsen, Director of the Opera House: 'He finds my new piece "exceedingly delightful"! . . . marvellous how one rises in their esteem! Before, one was just so much dirt'. The truth was that behind all this success lay a background of feverish work and concentrated thought which the public never dreamed of until the German text of these letters appeared in 1925.

No connoisseur of the Strauss operas from *Elektra* to *Arabella* can fail to be grateful for this faithful and fascinating account of the artistic progress of two geniuses, who met, corresponded and collaborated for nearly thirty years, but who never once in their letters addressed each other by their Christian names. That dignity and reserve may also have played its part in keeping their subtle artistic relationship on an even keel throughout storms and stresses not entirely of their own invention.

In general, correspondence about operas written during the past three centuries retains its validity and interest because the works themselves survive and can therefore be performed. A little further back in history, the situation changes: letters from Monteverdi to his various friends and patrons over the years 1601-43 that go into a wealth of detail about the composition, casting, and production of operas, ballets, masques, intermezzi, and tournaments whet the reader's appetite while failing to satisfy it, for most of the works discussed do not seem to have survived. Copies may turn up, of course, as they have often done in other areas of musical history, and if this should happen the correspondence will assume an added significance. As it stands, there is still much of value for the would-be interpreter of early Italian music of the baroque, and a little reading between the lines will add considerably to the general comprehension of a still largely unfamiliar period of lively development and experiment

With regard to the literary style of *Monteverdi's Letters* (London, 1980), it will be noticed at once that his flow of words not infrequently bears comparison with the best of his music. In many of the longer letters, there can be sensed that same white heat as from a creative crucible whose fusion of improvisation and formal discipline brought into being a taut masterpiece such as the *Combattimento* or the chaconne *Zefiro torna*. The subject is heard, soon to be enmeshed in the inexorable counterpoint of subsidiary themes, developed and extended by means of parenthetical allusions, with a return to the subject and the drive towards the final cadence. His letters in many ways mirror his music.

Apart from giving us a clear picture of the composer's

personality, as it developed over the last 42 years of his life, the letters reveal sharply-focussed details of his professional career, in addition to colourful vignettes of some of the musicians and courtiers he knew and with whom he collaborated. What results is a fascinating panorama of social conditions, especially in so far as they affected a busy musical director and composer working in Mantua, Venice, and Parma at a crucial time in the history of music. The span of the letters coincides with the burgeoning years of Italian opera and its associated forms and genres. We find here discussions of operatic aesthetics and problems of staging, matters pertaining to orchestration, the day-to-day relationship with patrons and librettists, not to mention the troubles and trials of duplicating full scores long before the days of photocopy.

Other letters, which frequently appear in groups, deal with such topics as the hiring of wind-players, the vocal ranges of singers (also their timbre and their skill in ornamentation); actors of the *commedia dell'arte* and their petty jealousies; alchemy as a kind of innocent hobby rather than a serious or full-time activity; the numerous worries attendant upon the education of sons in a city known for its libertine way of life; health and sickness as it affects creative work and travel; finance seen from many aspects – from that of the struggling composer, trying to make ends meet, and anxious for his just reward (part of which he never received), from the point of view of the ever-bargaining musician, whether singer or instrumentalist or instrument-maker, and from the later and loftier lookout-point of a successful man who can command considerable sums of money in special fees and commissions.

As for musical politics, Monteverdi is never hesitant to draw aside the curtains and show us what really went on in the courts and churches where, to the outsider, life must often have seemed to be beguilingly rosy. Rival factions, corrupt officials, back-biting and bad-mouthing, all can be seen with a clarity that is totally unflattering and sometimes frightening. Monteverdi is tricked by his employers, insulted by one of his musicians, forced to work at a pace that he does not relish; yet at other times he is happy with small successes – a helping hand from his sons, a concert that went well, a prestigious invitation to compose occasional music for a noble wedding.

Over and above the daily round, which might include a robbery at gunpoint or threats from the Inquisitor, there are generous portions of the letters that help us to understand what Monteverdi was doing as a musician. He mentions works that have survived – *L'Orfeo, Arianna, Il Combattimento, Tirsi e Clori* – and makes our ears tingle with accounts of lost works: *La finta pazza Licori*, probably the first comic opera; Mass and Vespers for Christmas in St Mark's; *Armida*, the parergon to *Il Combattimento*; stage works and ballets, madrigals and motets, canzoni and intermezzi; and fortunately there are some that can be identified with a reasonable degree of certainty even though their names to not appear – the two Petrarch madrigals from Book VI, the motet for the feast of Our Lady of Mont Carmel, the Intermezzi for *Le tre costanti*, the eight-part *Dixit Dominus* that was so often mis-quoted as being a five-part composition, and some of the motets for special feasts and occasions.

Observations of a comparable nature on passages in the correspondence of other composers cannot fail to add depth and meaning to a proper study of their music and their lives; for while it is obvious that background knowledge cannot substitute for the mechanics of technique in singing or playing, it can supply precious information capable of influencing the way in which a given piece of music is performed. One of the most important aspects of interpretation relates to tempo, for example, and the wrong tempi that one hears more often than not show a lack of familiarity on the part of the performer with the spirit of the age in which the composition was written. Once that spirit has been deliberately absorbed and understood, miscalculations are rare — technique finds itself in the service of higher considerations.

Periodicals and Related Ephemerides

The MGG article on periodicals (*Zeitschriften*), the greater part of which is given up to lists of past and present musical journals in dozens of different countries throughout the world, spreads itself in fine-printed fashion over 147 columns of that formidable dictionary; and parallel if less detailed accounts may be found in other major sources of reference. Why were all those trees cut down? The result, in any event, may strike the neophyte as little more than an impenetrable forest presided over by some brooding musicological Tapio, to whom sacrificial offerings are made with alarming frequency. For an author, the main problem is how to get in: how to get information out is the worry of the researcher.

While some periodicals provide annual indices, others are content to produce an index every forty or fifty years. In both cases the same difficulty crops up, because the information is non-cumulative and will eventually involve the curious in lengthy and time-consuming bouts with individual and limited alphabetical lists, unless of course a direct reference to volume number, year, and page has already been discovered. This is where the *Music Index* and *RILM* begin to be useful, though they are mainly concerned with articles and other sources of information in journals devoted primarily to music. What of the countless musical articles in other periodicals? The splendid library of the Society of Antiquaries in London has long maintained a special card-catalogue ordered by topics, and the music section of this extremely useful aid to research contains a considerable number of references to articles about music in non-musical journals.*

One would not normally look for materials on early English polyphony in the *Transactions of the Bristol and Gloucestershire Archaeological Society*, but Vol. 61 contains a vital link between the Spillman Cartulary and other,

*A recent and laudable attempt to improve matters is the 'Bibliographie der Aufsätze zur Musik in aussermusikalischen italienischen Zeitschriften' by Klaus Fischer, in *Analecta Musicologica* (Rome – Cologne).

far better known medieval sources. *The Modern Language Review* may not sound promising as a source for research into the music of 14th-century Germany, but Vol.XLVI features a valuable article about a song by the Minnesinger Wizlav von Rügen. Similarly, *Technology and Culture* would appear to restrict itself to scientific and sociological matters, but Vol.VII offers the organologist a fascinating account of keyboard mechanism in the late Middle Ages. *Speculum*, a journal of medieval studies published by the Mediaeval Academy of America (from 1926), has often given space to articles and reviews on early music. If you are looking for an authoritative survey of music in Quito from 1534 until 1934, the place to search is Vol.XLIII of *The Hispanic American Historical Review*. A brief but stimulating study of poetry and music in the *Air de Cour* turns up in Vol.2 of the *Forum for Modern Language Studies*. Largely unknown material on the music heard at the marriage of Philip II of Spain and Mary Tudor appears in Vol.XXII of the *Proceedings of the Hampshire Field Club*. An indispensable account of the musical collection of Edward Paston (1550-1630) is printed in Vol.IV of *Transactions of the Cambridge Bibliographical Society*.

It would not be difficult to add to the above list, for the back-log to which most musical periodicals are subject is so great that the publication of articles frequently suffers delay. Frustrated authors therefore turn to non-musical publications as new outlets for their work, but while this procedure is admirable from a practical point of view – as a means of unjamming intellectual traffic – it tends to make the researcher's life somewhat more complicated. One solution is to seek personal introductions to scholars working in the field that interests you: and having met them you can enquire where their latest articles have appeared. Gentle persistence may even result in the presentation of an offprint or two, for all authors enjoy distributing their works to those who seem most likely to appreciate such a gift.

Articles appear in all shapes and sizes. Most are genuine

and original contributions to scholarship, offering new discoveries or fresh viewpoints. They have come into being because their topic is too insubstantial for a book, and even if it became a small monograph the sales would perhaps be negligible. Publication in a scholarly journal, which reaches a relatively wide audience, is usually the best step: the article gets itself into circulation, and in the normal course of events will begin to turn up in the footnote references of other scholars within a decade. Occasionally an especially lengthy article, or a series of articles, will be reprinted as a monograph at the instance of the author, as in the case of Dragan Plamenac's *A Reconstruction of the French Chansonnier in the Biblioteca Colombina, Seville* (originally published in *The Musical Quarterly* as three articles, 1951-52) or Nino Pirrotta's *Scelte poetiche di Monteverdi*, which first saw the light in *Nuova Rivista Musicale Italiana*, 1968, as two instalments. It should be noted that in re-issues such as these, two sets of paginations often occur: that of the original publication, and that of the monograph; and these should be carefully distinguished if confusion is to be avoided.

While the best kind of article provides short-term research in a concentrated form, hopefully and preferably well-organized and written with some pretensions as to elegance and clarity of style, there is another kind that often shows up as padding, especially in the more scholarly journals. Such articles usually show signs of being hacked or sliced from a dissertation, and a casual glance at sister periodicals will reveal other hunks from the same dissertation by the same author. This is done in order to make the author's academic record of publication look impressively international, which in turn will help him towards promotion, tenure, or both. It may not necessarily help the reader, though in some instances, of course, extracts that have been suitably revised and re-written can and do stand on their own as worthy articles, but care should be exercised with regard to the other variety. More acceptable perhaps are the re-workings in article form of papers read at some convention or other, for while giving a lecture and writing an article really belong to two different disciplines, a skilled author can make the necessary adjustments in both directions and utilize materials in an oratorical or a literary manner.

The retrieval of information, much of which may turn up in the form of articles, is brought about by creating a list (or card-catalogue) of references found first in general then in particular works of scholarship and research; also in indexes compiled manually or by computer. Sometimes the resulting pile of materials looks almost too daunting to deal with, and in consequence the concept of 'total bibliographic control' starts to resemble the legend of the sorcerer's apprentice. Each newly-discovered article brings with it a collection of footnotes listing yet more articles, and the task becomes endless. In actual fact, much of this material consists of duplication, and an even larger quantity may be useless and outdated. The reason for this is that each contribution makes use of previously published material, and although ultimately the apex of the structure rests on a broad base, much of the supporting filler can, in certain circumstances, be set on one side and consulted only in case of need. As in the case of primary source-material, a stemma or diagram of filiation could be established in order to show how one article derives from several others, or from independent and original information.

It sometimes happens that a senior scholar collects together the best of his published articles and, at some culminating point in his career, re-issues them in the form of a book or even a multi-volume set. Mention may be made here of the two volumes of Friedrich Blume's writings (*Syntagma Musicologicum*) and three by Higini Anglés (*Scripta Musicologica*). This re-uniting of scattered materials can frequently be of great practical use to the researcher, who is thus able to study the articles in book form instead of hunting far and wide – often among very obscure and out-of-print serials – for elusive publications that may even turn out to be disappointing.

A related but much wider field is that of the Festschrift, usually a collection of tributes to a scholar by his colleagues and students. Although the articles contributed may reflect the interests of the person so honoured, there is a fair amount of freedom in general, with the result that the range of topics is frequently very wide. Some scholars, through a combination of renown and longevity, have qualified for more than one *Festschrift,* as witness three each for professors Helmut Osthoff and Charles van den Borren. One splendid volume – *Aspects of Medieval and Renaissance Music: A Birthday Offering to Gustave Reese* (New York, 1966) – contains an extremely useful 'Index of Festschriften and Some Similar Publications' by Walter Gerboth (pp. 183-307). It should also be borne in mind that a Festschrift sometimes appears as complete volume of an established periodical, such as that for Erich Schenk, as Vol.25 of *Studien zur Musikwissenschaft*; and for Nino Pirrotta, as Vol.X of *Rivista Italiana di Musicologia.*

Those musicians who are not habitually drawn to scholarship often find it hard to believe that periodicals and all that they contain still deserve detailed and careful study. It is highly dangerous to assume that the information contained in articles automatically finds its way into books on music and standard works of reference. Indeed the very opposite is frequently the norm. The guitarist who plays Montesardo's *La Monica* and the harpsichordist working on Frescobaldi's *Partite sopra lamonica* will search in vain for the explanation of these bizarre but obviously related titles – there is no entry for them in the established musical dictionaries in English, French, German, and Italian. But the mystery is solved for those performers who consult *Acta Musicologica* XLVIII (1976), 185-204, where John Wendland's study of the folksong 'Madre non mi far Monaca' places everything in clear perspective.

Some articles easily qualify as classics, though they may never have enjoyed any kind of career subsequent to their original publication. Manfred Bukofzer's brilliant essay on 'Interrelations between Conductus and Clausula', which first appeared in *Annales Musicologiques* I (1953), 65-104, ranks as a pioneering investigation of one of the more obscure areas in medieval music, throwing the light of fine scholarship on a topic that was seen through a glass darkly, if at all, and demonstrating with cool logic that early forms were not (as hitherto thought) self-contained and totally independent. Similarly, Nino Pirrotta's exemplary account of 'Marchettus de Padua and the Italian Ars Nova', in *Musica Disciplina* IX (1955), 57-72, remains by far the best source of information for this particular theorist and the age in which he lived.

Of special interest for those who perform medieval music is an article (in two parts) on 'Voices and Instruments in the music of Guillaume de Machaut', by Gilbert Reaney, in *Revue Belge de Musicologie* X (1956), 3-17; 93-104. Here, a well-known scholar and director of early music sets forth his views on the interpretation of Machaut's secular music, giving not only valuable advice but also well-founded cautions. Some of the distorted performances of early masterpieces performed and recorded today could have been avoided if those responsible had gone back to these basic articles, studied them, and heeded their suggestions. The music of Dufay's Roman period cannot be properly understood and performed without thorough knowledge of Heinrich Besseler's 'Dufay in Rom', best studied in *Miscelánea en homenaje a Mons. Higinio Anglés*, I (1958-61), 111-134, since the version of this article in *Archiv für Musikwissenschaft* 15 is abbreviated.

The art of organ playing and composing for the organ in the 15th century is a topic that leads to the Germany of Conrad Paumann, whose important treatise *Fundamentum organisandi* exerted an influence far outweighing its modest size. But its significance cannot be fully grasped unless the various and different versions are taken into consideration, compared, and collated – an exacting task that has never been satisfactorily accomplished in any accessible edition. For this reason it is necessary to refer to the article by Christoph Wolff: 'Conrad Paumanns Fundamentum organisandi und seine verschiedenen Fassungen', in *Archiv für Musikwissenschaft* XXV (1968), 196-222, where the problems are solved with expertise and insight.

Dance music in early times has long intrigued researchers and all those with terpsichorean tendencies. But where can one find a careful and detailed description of, say, 16th century court dances in Italy? No monograph or dictionary provides what we need, even though the treatises of Caroso and Negri – and their commentators – offer useful information about certain dances. Two Florentine manuscripts help to fill the gaps and expand our knowledge of the steps and music for four dances, and the steps (alas, without music) for 'La caccia'. They are fortunately transcribed by a most capable palaeographer, Gino Corti, in an article 'Cinque balli toscani del cinquecento', in *Rivista Italiana di Musicologia* XII (1977), 73-82. This is well worth the labour of translation.

All books on the history of music discuss the role of the poets and musicians of late 16th-century Florence – the so-called Camerata – with regard to dramatic music as it developed from a relatively simple adjunct into a well-established genre in its own right. But the problems of assessing the Camerata's contribution to the aesthetic doctrine and musical innovation of the movement have long deserved a re-assessment of their own. This is found in no monograph thus far published, but it does appear as a highly informative article by Claude V. Palisca: 'The "Camerata Fiorentina": A Reappraisal', in *Studi musicali* I (1972), 203-236. On the matter of early scores, in which much of this early vocal music was written down so that it could more easily be studied, there is no more helpful source than Edward E. Lowinsky's 'Early Scores in Manuscript', published with 24 photographic illustrations in the *Journal of the American Musicological Society* XIII (1960), 126-173. While it is by no means impossible that the author or one of his pupils might one day write a book on this fascinating topic, it could mean waiting for years, and in the meanwhile the article is the best way to find out all the basic information.

Certain types of research, by their very nature, exert only a very limited appeal even among scholars, and one of these is undoubtedly archival work. Obviously of great necessity in building up a basis for biographical and social studies, research into archives and transcription of the relevant material nevertheless has a limited audience, and book-length works in the field of music are rare. Many students of early English music who may be familiar with H.C. de Lafontaine's *The King's Musick* are not aware of a rich source of supplementary archival publications – those appearing in a long series of articles under the general title of 'Lists of the King's Musicians, from the Audit Office Declared Accounts', in *The Musical Antiquary* (all four extant volumes).

Documentary research also informs the thorough-going study of a famous prima donna – if the classical use of this term may be moved back to the 17th century – in Alberto Cametti's 'Chi era l' "Hippolita", cantatrice del cardinal di Montalto', in *Sammelbände der Internationalen Musikgesellschaft* XV (1913-14), 111-123. Who indeed was Hippolita? She seems to avoid the pages of standard reference works, if exception is made for a brief note 'Recupito, Ippolita: See *Canto*' in Ricordi's *Enciclopedia della Musica*. But her name changed from Recupito to Marotta when she married the composer and harpsichordist, Cesare Marotta, so that both names should be remembered when one looks for information about her career.

In the absence of a full-scale study of the interrelationship between folk music and art music, it may well be that scholars and musicians who are interested in this field will have to rely on articles for many years to come. To take only a very narrow topic— that of British folk song— it is perfectly clear that a number of composers whose national origins were far removed from England, Scotland, Wales, and Ireland found themselves drawn into this orbit thanks to the activities of George Thomson, the Edinburgh publisher of literary and musical contrafacta in the late 18th and early 19th century. He commissioned arrangements for voices and piano trio not only from minor figures (Kozeluch and Pleyel) but also from Haydn and Beethoven, who are even now not usually associated with such drawing-room trifles though they did not disdain to assist when the invitations arrived. Yet again, the standard works on Haydn and Beethoven tend to deal in summary fashion with this aspect of the two composers' work, so that recourse to detailed articles is the only answer to the problem. Fortunately there are five basic articles – Karl Geiringer: 'Haydn and the Folksong of the British Isles', in *The Musical Quarterly* XXXV (1949), 179-208; Alice Anderson Hufstader: 'Beethoven's Irische Lieder: Sources and Problems', in the same journal, XLV (1959), 343-360; then the two bibliographical studies by C.B. Oldman and Cecil Hopkinson – 'Thomson's Collections of National Song' and 'Haydn's Settings of Scottish Songs in the Collections of Napier and Whyte', in *Transactions of the Edinburgh Bibliographical Society* (1940; 1954); finally Donald McArdle's 'Beethoven and George Thomson' in *Music and Letters* XXXVII (1956), 27-49.

Even a brief listing such as the foregoing could be extended *ad infinitum*, taking on greater importance as we reach the present day, when criticism and discussion of contemporary music appears in newspapers and periodical literature long before it finds its way into books. The point to be emphasized is that articles sometimes contain valuable information not available elsewhere, and references should therefore be checked with care. Yet with all the help of an index or a print-out, the researcher with leisure hours to fill should occasionally indulge in the luxury of browsing through a set of periodicals and noting titles of interest so that they can be returned to at some future date. This may seem to be a long way around, but just as a circuitous ramble through the countryside often brings its own reward in terms of discovery, so it is with articles.

One other category deserves to be mentioned, since it

has been approved by many musicologists (including those of an earlier generation) as a worthy if humble adjunct to our source-materials: the gramophone record sleeve-note, or 'liner-note' in America. Not infrequently these useful sources of information are written by highly respected scholars who welcome the chance to bring together all the relevant and interesting facts about a given work, or programme of works, which are usually quite closely related to each other in view of the care with which recorded offerings are usually built. Moreover, they sometimes contain material not available in even the most obscure of scholarly articles, since there is a growing tendency to perform and record works before they are published. Some boxed sets often contain lavishly produced booklets with historical essays, illustrative material, and (in the case of vocal or choral works) complete texts and translations. Obviously the quality of these will vary according to the skills of contributors, but the standard is often astonishingly high and is much to the credit of the companies responsible. Maurice Maeterlinck was not far from the truth when he wrote, in the foreword to a programme of the Columbia Graphophone reception at the Théâtre des Champs-Elysées in 1928:

> Les plus hauts chefs-d'oeuvre du génie de l'homme reposent désormais à l'abri de la mort dans quelques disques, lourds de secrets spirituels, qu'un enfant de trois ans peut tenir dans ses petites mains.

Five

Collected Works and Musical Monuments

Two buxom young ladies of Trent,
Without the curator's consent,
Secreted six codices
Inside their bodices –
According to Edward J. Dent.

The above *rondeau cinquain*, anonymous in all sources but almost certainly of Neapolitan provenance, explains why it was necessary to discover a seventh codex in the lofty capital of the Alto Adige. And a codex (Latin for the trunk of a tree, from which the earliest books were fashioned) is nothing more than a manuscript containing text, illustrations, music – sometimes all three – of a generally valuable nature due to the unique and personal aspects of production. As every musicologist knows, the selections from the Trent Codices in modern notation form part of a series of *Denkmäler*: to be exact, *Denkmäler der Tonkunst in Österreich*, or Monuments of Music in Austria. From 1814 until 1918 Trent was part of the Austrian empire, and it was therefore logical to include this important source in a national series of monuments in 1900. Music is slow to adjust to changes in national boundary lines.

The art and science of making collected editions of music by a single composer, or collections of works by several composers, goes back far beyond our own century. Vincent Novello, founder of the publishing house that still bears the family name, edited numerous anthologies in the early years of the 19th century: his path-breaking four-volume edition of Purcell's sacred music (1826-32) was not the least of his achievements. A Handel Society formed in

Some Basic Materials

London in 1843 began but did not remotely reach completion of the collected works of that prolific composer, who was taken under the wing of a second society, the Händel-Gesellschaft, formed in Germany with massive support in 1856. In the meantime Schumann and others had successfully launched the Bach-Gesellschaft in 1850, beginning a half-century of notable activity in the publication of comparable series of collected works.

Nor was the other side of the coin neglected by those energetic if untutored musicologists of the romantic era. Early baroque music from Italy was edited and discussed by Carl von Winterfeld in his *Johannes Gabrieli und sein Zeitalter* (3 vols., 1834); Elizabethan composers and Purcell emerged from obscurity in the 19 volumes of the Musical Antiquarian Society (1840-47); choral music by 16th-century Netherlanders filled the 12 volumes of the *Collectio operum musicorum batavorum saeculi XVI* edited by the organist and composer Franz Commer from 1844 until 1858; a slightly later set of 10 volumes enlarged the same repertoire thanks to the efforts of Karl Proske (an army doctor who became a priest and musician) and his assistants in their *Musica Divina*. Devotees of the keyboard were able to explore a wide range of unfamiliar music issued in 23 volumes as *Le Trésor des pianistes* by Jacques and Jeanne Louise Farrenc (1861-72); another treasury, this time of sacred and secular vocal music, was compiled and published between 1865 and 1893 by R.J. van Maldéghem as *Trésor musical* (a reprint contains a valuable index and introduction by Gustave Reese, 1974); and Robert Eitner's *Publikation älterer praktischer und theoretischer Musikwerke* of 29 volumes, began in 1873, carried over into the present century a remarkable collection of works by French, German, Italian, and Netherlandish masters.

These are but chips off the block of musicological achievement in the nineteenth century, which simply carried on with even greater energy what had been established in earlier times. Much earlier, in fact, for were not the main

manuscripts of medieval organum and conductus (especially those associated with libraries in Florence and Wolfenbüttel) nothing more than hand-written *Denkmäler*? If
so, then countless collections of this kind should be so
regarded, for the Old Hall Manuscript provides a generous
sampling of liturgical polyphony, mainly English, from the
late fourteenth and early fifteenth centuries, while the
Trent Codices do the same on an even grander scale thanks
to the patronage and collector's curiosity of Bishop Johann
Hinderbach. Much later, and in printed form, William
Boyce assembled and edited what he considered to be the
best of English church music in his three volumes of
Cathedral Music (1760-78). As far as *Gesamtausgaben* are
concerned, perhaps Machaut was the earliest of the great
composers to supervise the collection, ordering, and
illumination of his own complete works, if the evidence of
the best of his manuscripts in the Bibliothèque Nationale
can be trusted, as it generally is. Nor is the vast expanse of
early printed music without its examples of this concern, on
the part of serious composers, for seeing at least some
considerable portion of their work circulating in reasonably correct copies.

Whatever happened in earlier centuries, our own has
much to answer for when we come to assess its contribution
to the unearthing, transcribing, editing, and publishing of
early music. The great composers having been resuscitated
in their serried ranks of heavy tomes, it then became the
scholar's duty to deal with the less than great; and as the
gigantic barrel was scraped to its very bottom so that the
complete or collected works of almost totally unknown
composers could appear for the first time in score, the
bottom collapsed and the entire contingent vanished into
another barrel beneath the first one. If one musicologist in
one lifetime sees an average of fifty students through their
PhDs, and if those in turn produce an equal or greater
number of comparably gifted researchers, it follows that
the amount of music now being quarried from European
libraries – in partial fulfilment of degree requirements and

in total disregard of whether it will ever serve some useful purpose – has reached truly gigantic proportions. Much of it will, of course, be useful as long as there are choirs, orchestras, and early music groups seeking novel repertoire, for it is they who will introduce secular audiences to the masses of motets and the innumerable Masses originally written for sacred ends, in the same way that they will perform madrigals, chansons, dance-music and concertos for the ever-curious connoisseur.

The basic fact most frequently lost sight of in all this activity relates quite simply to aesthetic quality. Much of the music now being re-published has little enough claim to a high intrinsic standard of excellence, since it was often written for purely functional ends and without any concern on the part of the composers for historical longevity – indeed many of them, brought back to life by some miracle or other, would be astounded to find their humble contributions re-issued in the form of luxuriously printed full scores to which all manner of critical apparatus has been added in an earnest endeavour to convert art into science. On the other hand, the great virtue of such editions is to enable musicians of today, unskilled perhaps in the deciphering of early source-material, to read through with comparative ease a vast quantity of repertoire some of which may prove of interest to them in building programmes for concerts or records. Over and above this minor consideration, it should always be recognized that genuine scholarship is an end in itself, and that quality or usefulness can generally be relegated to musical limbo.

Collected Works of Individual Composers

The best comprehensive guide is Anna H. Heyer's *Historical sets, collected editions and monuments of music*, first published in 1967 (Chicago, American Library Association) and constantly updated. Dictionary lists given under such headings as *Gesamtausgaben* and *Collected Works* are reliable only in so far as their date of compilation allows: the entry in MGG vol.4 was published in 1955, and its compilation may have ended in 1953. Since that date, new editions of the works of various composers have begun to replace the old sets, while newly-begun projects dealing with composers hitherto unrepresented among the collected works series have taken firm root and are now well under way. Publishing houses are sometimes thoughtful enough to prepare special booklets listing sets in print and in progress, and what is more they show exemplary generosity in supplying these booklets free of charge. Bärenreiter produces a *Monumenta musica* catalogue, and an even more ambitiously planned publication comes from Broude Brothers Ltd (56 West 45th Street, New York, N.Y. 10036), covering collected editions, historical sets, reference works, monographs, and periodicals.

A well-equipped library usually has its collected works shelved in alphabetical order of the composers, which gives the neophyte researcher an easy start. It will soon be found, however, that the spines of these bulky volumes rarely disclose any information regarding their actual content, thus making it necessary to consult a 'second knowledge' catalogue. Some of the old Breitkopf and Härtel editions – such as Palestrina and Bach – offer useful lists of incipits and thematic indices in the final volume, but the newer editions cannot yet do so because they are still incomplete. The more comprehensive dictionaries provide detailed information about the contents of each set, and in some cases there are two ways of approaching it – either in numerical order of the volumes (Bach article in MGG 1, cols. 1039-1041), or according to genre (*Gesamtausgaben* article in MGG 4, col. 1854). A modern thematic index, if one is available, should supersede all other guides and abbreviated lists.

It is worth-while bearing in mind that the older collected editions – Josquin, Schütz, Palestrina, Handel, and many more – made extensive use of C-clefs in various positions on the staff, especially for solo voices and chorus, whereas the modern sets tend to restrict themselves to treble and bass clefs in that respect. In addition, the scholarship and accuracy of older editions is often questionable in the light of modern research. Those courageous attempts to assemble a reasonably complete corpus of works by one composer nevertheless continue to serve as material for quick reference; and in libraries where it is comparatively easy to consult them for rapid reading, programme building, and similar ends, their usefulness should not be ignored. Nor should it be assumed automatically that a new set is always and in every respect better than an old one, for the new Handel Edition contains some reliable volumes and others that leave much to be desired in the matter of collating printed and manuscript sources. The right technique to develop and use should be based on comparison: by all means consult what is most easily available, but try if possible to compare what you have with what may be available elsewhere – even in a practical performing edition.

In this colossal acreage of tertiary materials (music produced with the performer in mind) the primary problem is to orient oneself correctly and ascertain if possible whether a given edition is based on a reliable secondary source – collected edition or monument as the case may be – by comparing the two. Separate bibliographies have been compiled for vocal, choral, and instrumental music of all kinds, ranging over the entire history of music, and their titles may be found under the general heading 'Bibliographies of Music' in the latest edition of *Music Reference and Research Materials* by Vincent Duckles. There is a short cut, however, and that is to consult first of all the series of catalogues published by the British Broadcasting Corporation in London. Covering all genres and all periods, they index each work in alphabetical order of composers, with details of scoring, approximate duration (based on studio timings) and publisher. Although this remarkable assemblage of performing materials does not rank as a lending library, the ease with which catalogues can be consulted is a major factor in establishing it as a reliable starting-point for further research.

When a general catalogue gives information about publishers, due note should be taken, for a hint or clue of this kind tells you where to look for further work by a composer, be he ancient or modern. It is true, of course, that since the beginnings of music publishing countless composers have proved themselves to be more prolific than the presses that turn out their work, and they have often had recourse to the ploy of working with more than one publisher. Modern composers are no exception to the rule. But once the names of a composer's principal publishers have been discovered, it is not difficult to request copies of the particular catalogues (choral, orchestral, piano, or whatever), and so build up a total *oeuvre* the details of which can then be filed away for reference.

Historical Sets and Monuments of Music

These categories tend to be more troublesome for the researcher since they are often open-ended, so that reference works – usually a few years behind the times – can only index the volumes in print at the time of compilation. Newer volumes have to be studied and analysed separately. Once again, however, the best guide is the Heyer volume mentioned earlier (p.74). There is also a useful breakdown of the principal *Denkmäler* under the heading 'Editions, Historical' in the *Harvard Dictionary of Music*. The list in Grove VI (1980) is even more up-to-date. Those who have access to the *Rivista Italiana di Musicologia* will find a comprehensive listing, by Alberto Basso, of monuments, anthologies, and collections in Vol.VI (1971), 3-135. What these three last-mentioned accounts need is an index of composers, for unless a fuller reference is at hand it may be necessary to browse or burrow in order to find out what is required.

The value of variegated anthologies – which is what the *monumenta* really amount to – resides in their unique and special way of bringing together diverse works by different composers and yet preserving some common bond or category. National series serve as their own guides, for if the musician is looking for German music he will not be disappointed in the German, Austrian, and Bavarian *Denkmäler* and their offshoots — though this is not to say that he will fail to make the acquaintance of Italian music (DDT 55, 60; DTB 1, 16, 21, 23; DTÖ 6, 9, 20, 110) since so many southern composers made their way to northern courts and climates because of the opportunities for lavish music-making paid for in hard currency. The English, French, Italian, Spanish, Polish, Czech and other series of this kind normally keep to their own national composers, though there are some minor exceptions.

Building a programme for a concert, or for a recording, is thus made comparatively easy, for the mere floating of an idea such as 'The English Madrigal', 'Instrumental Music in 16th-century Spain', or 'Viennese Church Music under the later Habsburgs' sends one immediately to the national series in question. In the reverse direction, it is not uncommon for the title of a volume to suggest an area of study or performance, such as 'Music in Catalonia up to the 13th century' (Biblioteca de Catalunya: *Publicaciones*, Vol.10); 'Carnival Songs of the Renaissance' (*Das Chorwerk*, Vol.43); 'Fourteenth-century Mass Music in France' (*Corpus mensurabilis musicae*, Vol.29); 'Thuringian Motets from the first half of the 18th century' (DDR Vols.49-50); 'Latin motets in France, 1609-1661' (*Publications de la Société française de musicologie*, Vol.17). The list could clearly be extended, even if not *ad infinitum*.

What is sorely needed for this growing mass of material is a special bibliographical tool, produced with the aid of a computer, offering such facilities as a complete list of composers whose works are found in miscellaneous collections and musical monuments; a complete list of incipits; and a grouping of compositions by genres – opera, oratorio, fantasia, concerto, motet, or whatever broad and detailed sub-headings as may be required to make research straightforward and unencumbered. Until this comes about, the old-fashioned methods will have to serve as best they can.

Facsimile Editions

At present there appears to be no reliable index to facsimiles, despite the fact that excerpts from early printed and manuscript sources were published even before the days of photography. Perhaps such an index is even now in course of publication, and when issued it will fill a gap in music bibliography. Certainly there is no entry for 'Facsimile Editions' in the great dictionaries, although they themselves feature pages in black-and-white or colour, illustrating articles on composers, notation, forms, or sources. Facsimiles produced on a lavish scale cover almost every area of musical history, from the early chant manuscripts in *Paléographie musicale* to the full score of Gilbert and Sullivan's *The Mikado*. Some modern compositions are reproduced from the composer's manuscript, and may therefore be placed in the general category of facsimile editions.

What the facsimile does is to allow scholars and musicians to study and verify the notation (and text, if any) as written by the composer in a sketch, a fair copy for his own use, or a copy for the use of a printer-publisher. Even the most careful transcriptions contain errors, and a transcription inevitably reflects some of the judgements and prejudices of the scholar responsible: it follows therefore that a comparison of source and edition may sometimes reveal unsuspected subtleties that could have an important effect on interpretation. It is advisable to find out whether a facsimile of a work exists before sending away for a microfilm, since the ease with which the former can be consulted is one of the prime reasons for its production, quite apart from its artistic or historical significance.

When a single work forms the basis of a facsimile, an index is obviously superfluous; but when (for instance) an outstanding early source of the 'monumental' variety lies before us, our first need is for an expert guide. Surprisingly, many facsimiles are published without even the most basic and elementary index to help the reader find what he wants. Fortunately, however, scholars come to the rescue and provide inventories such as those listed in Chapter Three, so that when the facsimile and the inventory are used together everything begins to make better sense. Sometimes an index appears separately in the form of a booklet, as in the case of *An Old St. Andrews Music Book* (London, 1931) for which Dom Anselm Hughes supplied an Index in 1939; sometimes it forms part of an article or review in a periodical, as with Martin Picker's Index to the Dijon Chansonnier in *Journal of the American Musicological Society* XXVI (1973), 337-340 — reviewing the facsimile of Dijon, Bibliothèque publique, Ms.517 (Institute of Medieval Music, Brooklyn, [1971]).

If it can be safely assumed that by far the greater number of facsimiles are published as bound volumes, occasional exceptions to this custom should be noted, as for example the complete facsimile of the Faenza Codex, which was reproduced (without an index!) in *Musica Disciplina* Vols. 13, 14, and 15 (1959-1961). It is not unusual to meet with a high quality facsimile in a single volume or a set of volumes dealing with one source, and as an example of the former kind one might mention Richard R. Terry's edition of *Calvin's First Psalter* (London, 1932) containing preface, facsimile, transcription, and performing edition; of the latter the three-volume edition of *The Medici Codex* by Edward E. Lowinsky (Chicago, 1968). In addition to the musical organizations that sponsor facsimiles of unique and special sources, one sometimes encounters exemplary generosity in private foundations, such as the Robert Owen Lehman Foundation of Washington, D.C., which distributed to libraries a remarkable series of facsimile editions, among them major works by Mozart, Beethoven, Brahms, Chopin, and Debussy.

Critical Apparatus

Musicians frequently encounter difficulties when they wish to question editorial readings based on the interpretation of a single source where the notation is obscure or problematic, or of more than one source where it has been necessary to choose the most satisfactory version. What if the notation, when transcribed, is still not convincing? What if the choice of a particular reading leaves something to be desired? In normal circumstances the scholar will list methodically all deviations from the original(s) so that those who work with the edition can, if they so wish, make up their own minds in matters of dispute. The main point to bear in mind is that no commonly-accepted standard exists in the setting forth of critical apparatus, a term usually recognizable in languages other than English: *Notes critiques, Revisione critica, Crítica de la edición, Revisionsbericht*. Each editor tends to invent his own method, or take over a pre-existing one to which he may make additions or modifications. The reader must therefore ascertain at first how the apparatus works, and this can be done by studying the abbreviations used, as well as the method of referring to particular lines and bars in the score. Three quite different approaches are explained in the following paragraphs, dealing with music of the 14th, 16th, and 18th centuries respectively.

1. *La cappella musicale del duomo di Milano. Parte prima — Le origini e il primo maestro di cappella: Matteo da Perugia.* Editor, Fabio Fano. (Milan, 1956.) This volume is the first in a new series of *Istituzioni e monumenti dell'arte musicale italiana*, and its musical transcriptions range over the sacred and secular music of Matteo da Perugia, some anonymous works by his contemporaries, and a single work by Beltrame Feragut. In the critical apparatus (pp.409-475), the editor concentrates on notational questions, and since he is concerned with one principal manuscript source, the collation of material and comparison of readings hardly enter into this section of the book. The approach is mainly technical and the questions raised often affect the reading and performance of the music. Note that the abbreviations used are given not at the beginning of the critical apparatus, but on p. 170.

v

Some Basic Materials

The example chosen relates to [*Gloria* . . .] *Et in terra*, No.2 – music: pp. 196-205; notes: pp.412-417. This particular reference is to p. 416, where the note on bar 102 reads as follows in the original —

'B. 102, *Sup*.: manca il *p.div*. prima della min., per cui a rigore questa andrebbe aggregata alla semib. precedente, che essa renderebbe imperfetta *a parte post*. Ma l'imperfezione della longa *a parte ante* e *quoad partem remotam* sembra una della caratteristiche del *superius* di questo brano: inoltre il testo ci suggerisce la correzione, essendo la sillaba *bis* collocata sotto il *do* e non potendo star bene che in principio di battuta'.

This may be translated:

Bar 102, Alto: 'The point of division before the minim is lacking, which (because of this) should rightly be grouped with the preceding semibreve, which it would make imperfect by a following note. But the imperfection of the long by a preceding note, and as far as a note of the third-following degree, seems to be one of the characteristics of the alto part in this composition; besides which the text suggests the correction to us, since the syllable *bis* is placed beneath the C and cannot be right except at the beginning of the bar'.

All this can best be explained by reference to the music. Strictly speaking, the note-group semibreve-minim-long (shown just above each stave) should be transcribed as in Ex.3a; but the editor, basing his opinion on stylistic considerations, realized that the minim that goes with the syllable *bis* ought to be on a strong beat, and he therefore assumed that the point of division had been omitted by the scribe. The conjectural original notation, with revised transcription, appears in Ex.3b. It goes without saying that note-values are quartered in both transcriptions.

Ex.3(a,b)

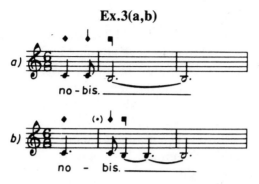

The above examples are disarmingly simple since they give the initial impression of concordance between old and new notations, whereas in fact the mischievous dot means different things at different times. In the Middle Ages, one of its uses was to set off one time-unit from another, whereas in more recent times it served to add on half the value of the note it followed, a usage still recognized today.

2. *Harmonice Musices Odhecaton A*. Editor, Helen Hewitt. (Cambridge, Mass., 1942.) An outstanding edition of a famous example of early music-printing, in which most of the compositions are compared with important manuscript sources in order to show significant variants. The editor explains the *modus operandi* of her critical apparatus on p. 183, and the list of manuscripts (referred to by such abbreviations as F 59, FP, SG 1) begins on p. 105. Our example is Compère's four-part chanson *Un franc archier* (Odhecaton No. 28), with music on pp. 279-280, and critical notes on p. 190. Variants in the tenor part, which is untexted, appear as follows:

> T m10:4ff, A sbr; m21:2ff, G sbr, F min; m27:1ff, D 2 min; m31:4ff, no flat before E; m45:1ff, A min, G min, A, B smin, C, D, B min, C sbr

This list of variants, like those for (S)uperius, (A)ltus, (B)assus, is printed below the siglum F 59, which refers to a manuscript dated about 1500 in Florence, Biblioteca Nazionale Centrale (Ms XIX, 59). It tells us the following:

Tenor: measure (bar) 10, fourth beat (and following note) is A semibreve. M.21, second beat (and following) is G semibreve, F minim. M.27, first beat (and following), D minim, D minim. M.31, fourth beat (and following), no flat before E (but the player of this part would have sounded E flat anyway, in accordance with the rules of musica ficta). M.45, first beat (and following), A minim, G minim, A semiminim, B semiminim, C minim, D minim, B minim, C semibreve.

In order to fit the original note-values, as given in this list, to those of the transcriptions, they must be halved so that semibreve becomes our modern minim (half-note); minim becomes our crotchet (quarter-note); semiminim becomes our quaver (eighth-note). Translated into notation, we have:

Ex. 4

The variants for bars 10, 21, and 27 affect only the melody, not the harmony, while that for bar 31 affects the harmony only if the player is a dimwit. Bars 45 and 46, in the MS version, are harmonically impossible, causing consecutive fifths as well as wrong notes. It may well be asked why the scholar bothers to record so meticulously something that is clearly at fault, since it cannot be seriously taken into consideration as a possible variant reading as far as performance is concerned. The answer is that it is part of the discipline to record everything, right or wrong, because there are times when even a wrong reading can teach us something about the place a manuscript has in a *stemma*, or hypothetic complex of sources that shows how one scribe copied from another.

3.   Gluck: *Paride ed Elena*. Opera in five acts; libretto by Calzabigi. Editor, Rudolf Gerber. (Kassel and Basel, 1954.) This volume, or rather double volume, is the fourth in the series devoted to operatic works in the collected works of Gluck published under the aegis of the Institute for Musical Research in Berlin. In the list of sources (p. 309) the original score published in 1770 is stated to be the most reliable since no autograph is extant: all manuscript copies of the score, as of the orchestral, choral and solo parts derive from the edition of 1770. Since many of these copies were used for actual performances, markings of one kind or another reflect the practices and customs of conductors, instrumentalists, and singers in the late 18th and early 19th centuries. To this extent they may accordingly be of some value today, and the editor has collated them in a twenty-page critical apparatus.

The list of libraries containing copies of the full score of 1770 should be augmented to show that the Hirsch copy is now in the British Library (formerly British Museum), where in addition to the copy listed there is another in the King's Library. A further exemplar may be seen in the Pendlebury Library, Cambridge, and doubtless others have come to light since 1954.

Some Basic Materials

Our example is taken from Act II – the aria of Paride (Paris), 'Le belle immagini d'un dolce amore', which is accompanied by oboes, bassoons, strings and continuo (pp. 100-108). The critical notes on this aria appear on p. 318, column 3, and p. 319, cols. 1 and 2. For reasons of space, the annotations following deal only with p. 100:

> 100-108 – Bogen, Staccato und Dynamik in den Hss. nur spärlich angedeutet.
> L₁ – die Achtelgruppen ♪♪♪♪ in allen Instr. stets ohne Bogen. Die Überschrift "Andante grazioso" fehlt.
> 100 – 1 – Viol. I, II, Va – L₁ P W₁ – piano: dgl. T. 5 in P W₁ W₂.
> 100 – 2,4,6,8 – Viol.I, II – W₁ W₂ – auf der 1. Note sf; T.2, 6 auf der 4. Note piano. Ebenso T. 2,6 in P. In P W₂ T.4, 8 sf. auf der 3. Note.
> 100 – 9 – Viol.I – P W₁ W₂ – piano.
> 100 – 9 – Bässe – L₁ W₂ W₂ – ohne piano.

The above tells us:

Pp.100-108 (that is, throughout the entire aria) slurs, staccato-marks, and dynamics are shown only occasionally in the manuscripts. In London, British Library, RCM Ms. 2050, the quaver-groups ♪♪♪♪ in all instruments are always without slurs. The tempo-mark 'Andante grazioso' is lacking.

P.100, bar 1, Violins 1, 2, Violas (in London, BL, RCM 2050; Paris, Bibliothèque Nationale, Vm⁴ 49; Vienna, Gesellschaft der Musikfreunde), are marked *piano*. The same goes for bar 5 in the last two sources, also in Vienna, Nationalbibliothek MS 17781.

P.100, bars 2,4,6,8, Violins 1, 2 (in the two Vienna MSS just cited), *sforzando* marks on the first note. In bars 2 and 6, *piano* on the fourth note. The same for bars 2 and 6 in the Paris MS. Bars 4 and 8 the Paris MS and Vienna Nationalbibliothek MS have *sforzando* on the third note.

P.100, bar 9, Violins I (the Paris and both Vienna MSS),
   piano.
P.100, bar 9, Basses (the London and both Vienna MSS
   cited), no *piano*.

The effect of these markings on the score would be as
follows:

Ex. 5

By way of conclusion, it should again be stressed that each editor organizes his critical apparatus in his own way, and however derivative the basic elements may be, their appearance in a larger context makes it necessary to study and understand the procedure completely if one is to get the most out of these algebraically cabalistic tables of variants. As with so many other aspects of musical scholarship, industry and perseverance bring their own reward – not a large one, perhaps, but frequently useful and always enlightening.

Part Three

Applied Musicology

Six

The Presence of Early Music

'It is otherwise with old music . . . one cannot hear it for the first time. Some magic of reminiscence haunts the ear.'
H.N. Brailsford: *Adventures in Prose*

There exists today a small but fortunately not very influential coterie of individuals who appear to be suffering from the delusion that they have 'invented' early music and are solely responsible for its present cultivation, inextricably entwined as it is with *Musealer Klangmaterialismus*. This term, coined by Hans Redlich in 1936, 'denotes the tendency of some modern arrangers of old music to restore it according to the letter rather than to the spirit, by using obsolete and historical instruments'. A pedantic and impoverished performance of a Bach fugue on the harpsichord is not necessarily superior to an adequate rendition on the piano, but given a first-rate performance of the same work on either piano or harpsichord we may, if we are honest with ourselves, admit that it is sometimes hard to choose between the two media.

Earlier enthusiasts for early music rarely had authentic historical instruments at their disposal, though there were notable exceptions, as when Moscheles, in the first of a series of 'pianoforte evenings' in February 1837, played several compositions by Scarlatti on a harpsichord. Liszt, when playing Scarlatti, contented himself with the piano, as did Mendelssohn and Hiller when they joined him in a performance of a Bach Triple Concerto in Leipzig, early in 1840, at the Gewandhaus. When Anton Rubinstein gave a series of farewell recitals in London during May and June, 1886, he was warmly applauded for his interpretations – on the piano – of Scarlatti, Byrd, Bull, Couperin, Rameau, and C.P.E. Bach.

This is not to condone completely such performances, or countless others like them uncatalogued and unremembered; quite clearly we now know better. Nevertheless, distortion is not limited to one kind or manner, as we shall see later. The main point to remember is that even a modest attempt to trace the history of early music revivals would call for a book of considerable size and scope, in which credit should be given to those active in the field prior to the 1970's. Proof that precursors are often ignored may be seen in an article ('Return of Early Forms', *The Daily Telegraph*, 12 August 1978) by Robert Henderson, a critic who wrote a thesis on a medieval topic. Yet even he maintains that 'twenty years ago early music still belonged almost exclusively to the scholar and archivist', and that 'scores, whether of modern transcriptions or facsimiles, were rare, expensive, and mostly inaccessible'.

But in 1958 (and well before) there was already an enthusiastic audience for pre-classical repertoire thanks not only to the BBC's Third Programme, on which early music and instruments were frequently heard, but also to the notable though less bountiful contributions from the recording and concert world. Listeners, collectors, and audiences were very rarely scholars and archivists, but rather members of a growing new public satiated with music of the 19th century. Similarly with scores: for if we restrict the field to England alone, and to one particular series, the first fifteen volumes (1951-58) of *Musica Britannica* included several devoted to vocal and instrumental repertoire prior to 1600. Moreover they were easily obtainable, practical as well as scholarly, and gave good value for a reasonable and moderate price, which is more than can be said for some of the musical monuments produced today, when high production costs tend to bring about dauntingly inflated selling prices.

Let us be grateful then to the various good examples set by London's Antient Concerts (1776-1848), where the music usually had to have matured more than twenty years in the cask; Germany's Cecilian Movement, which did so much to revive liturgical polyphony of the Renaissance; and the Société des Concerts de Musique Religieuse et Classique, founded by Adolphe Adam and the Prince de la Moskowa, echoes of whose ever-enterprising programmes occur in sources such as the correspondence of the painter Henri Lehmann and Countess Marie d'Agoult. In a letter dated 28 May 1844 he mentions one of those concerts, at which 'a four-part chanson of the 16th century entitled *Fuyons tous d'amour le jeu*' was sung; though whether this was the fugacious setting by Lasso or the chordal one by Certon is not specified.

We should also remember, for the most part thankfully, the many composers who unselfishly gave of their time to help the cause of their worthy predecessors – Mendelssohn's tireless promotion of Bach, and his deep interest in Palestrina and Mozart; the editorial work of Saint-Saëns on behalf of Rameau, Gluck, and Marc-Antoine Charpentier; Busoni's interest in Monteverdi's *Ritorno d'Ulisse* and the madrigals. While Vaughan Williams was working in London on an edition of Purcell's odes, Anton von Webern as a young Ph.D. in musicology busied himself with a scholarly transcription of part of Isaac's *Choralis Constantinus* in Vienna. In more recent times, the composer who did most to foster the knowledge and performance of early music (albeit in the limited circle of Yale University) was Paul Hindemith, and those who admire this aspect of his work – or who wish to correct their own possible misunderstanding of the early music syndrome – could do no better than to read the fascinating account of one of his students, Eckhart Richter, whose article 'Paul Hindemith as Director of the Yale Collegium Musicum' appears in *College Music Symposium* 18 (1978), 20-44.

The cultivation of early music is not, therefore, a recent phenomenon. But it would be true to say that the amount of research into all pre-classical fields and the publication of editions both monumental and practical have increased by leaps and bounds – and have sometimes gone well beyond bounds – in the years following World War II; so that the sheer size of the repertory is such that one lifetime seems hardly enough to take it all in. Although Curt Sachs considered that certain kinds of editing did little more than transfer old music from one graveyard to another, the invention and perfection of inexpensive photo-copying has played an important role in the concept of 'instant early music', whereby anybody can put together a group of performers and keep them constantly supplied with materials copied (more often than not without permission or acknowledgment) from volumes that represent years of a scholar's life and a heavy investment by some altruistic publisher.

If the leader of an ensemble is a trained musical palaeographer and editor, accustomed to preparing scores and parts from original sources, he can be relied upon to supply proper documentation and whatever acknowledgment may be deemed appropriate; but this is unfortunately very rare. Most ensembles simply help themselves to what is available, well aware for the most part that hard-working editors are not usually in a position to claim copyright either in its basic form – the right to copy – or in such ancillary rights as might be covered by performance, recording or broadcasting. If an element of copyright can be claimed by reason of a written-out continuo part or a clearly specified manner of orchestration, it can just as easily be denied by stating that the harpsichordist did not make use of the published realization, and that the conductor made up a different orchestration from that supplied in the score.

More often than not a reference to the editor or his publisher is a matter of conscience or courtesy rather than a legal obligation, yet it is greatly to be hoped that as the early music movement grows and flourishes, its exponents will cast off their corsair image and follow the example of the scholarly world, where sources are meticulously cited and assistance duly acknowledged.*

One of the most remarkable features of the early music movement is its sensitivity to fashion. Not only do different facets of the repertoire alternately glimmer and recede: modes of performance come and go, like the ensembles that launch them. Records issued over the past twenty-five years tell a tale of their own, as may be gauged from reading the two excellent articles by Elizabeth Roche (*The Musical Times* cxx [1979], January and March); and if the pre-LP era were ever to be investigated anew, even more surprising facts would emerge. A virtually unknown essay on this subject, written by a scholar to whom all devotees of early music are perforce indebted – Dr Armen Carapetyan, founder and editor-in-chief of the American Institute of Musicology – repays in ample measure the trouble of seeking it out from *Musica Disciplina* XXV (1971) where it appears as an Editorial: 'Some Remarks on Current Performance of Early Music'.

Dr Carapetyan finds that too many recorded performances are 'outright offensive' or leave the listener 'disappointed or dissatisfied'. He blames record companies for ignorance, bad judgment or poor taste; yet it is only fair to point out that they usually do no more than place their trust in a certain director or ensemble in the expectation that due preparation will have been made long before the actual recording takes place. He also blames the economic factor, which is by no means negligible when it comes to the computation of rehearsals and sessions. Many a director would welcome one per cent of the studio time allocated to the spawning of the latest rock album; yet the bizarre

*In the course of recording several Monteverdi programmes for the BBC in 1966, I found that the *Gloria concertata a 7* was so little known that chorus parts and orchestral material did not exist in the Music Library. I therefore orchestrated the work in accordance with documentary evidence relating to the first performance under Monteverdi's direction, and the material was duly placed in the library, where the card-index reflected my editorial work. Almost at once it was taken out by another conductor and recorded commercially, and since then by countless others, all of whom have courteously refrained from any mention of the responsible editor.

business tenets of a massive organization gorged upon the profits of those albums rarely if ever allow one of its minuscule sub-companies selling early music to benefit from the surplus. Each enterprise must pay its way; and the successful cannot be expected to subsidize those records enjoying only a modest sale.

In the course of his further objurgations and animadversions, Dr Carapetyan mentions poor balance between a flute and harpsichord; two versions of a Josquin Mass – one purist, pale, thin in sonority, the other full of sudden contrasts in timbre and dynamics – neither of which does justice to the work; a disc devoted to the music of Giovanni Gabrieli which ranks as 'a frightful insult to a glorious composer'; and examples of 'bellowing' in a record of English carols. *Sic transit gloria* Jean-Pierre Rampal, Les chanteurs de Saint-Eustache, The Texas Boys' Choir, New York Pro Musica; and if the sacred cows of the 1970s are thus rejected, woe betide their successors in office.

In a single issue of *The Musical Times* – cxix (1978), November – three different critics express their frustration and annoyance on hearing the Concentus Musicus of Vienna, a group which has done good work on occasion even though it is often subject to manneristic extremism. In a record of Bach Cantatas, Robert Anderson finds the strings sounding 'as unvocal as possible, phrasing in snuffles and sneezes, while the voices are allowed to avoid infection as best they can. This may be the ultimate in authenticity: it certainly makes uneasy listening and allows the faithless to sympathize with Bach's distress at the performing practice of his time'. Commenting on the same group in a Handel recording, Anthony Hicks draws our attention to a habit of 'snapping violently at isolated chords' and a fondness for 'quite large dynamic gradations within a phrase' and generally quirky phrasing. Finally, Winton Dean's evaluation of their version of Monteverdi's *Orfeo* mentions a method of handling voices 'that punctuates the vocal line with bleats, gasps and whispers descending almost to *Sprechgesang*, with lamentable effect on Monteverdi's subtle and flexible arioso'. As far as the orchestra goes, he finds that 'the mixture of fastidious scholarship in the instruments themselves with its opposite in their employment' is disturbing.

Similarly, a single issue of *Records and Recording* – 21 (1978), July – demonstrates a clear reaction against *Musealer Klangmaterialismus* on the part of three intelligent and unprejudiced critics. Arthur Hutchings prefers the *Forty-Eight* 'on a piano rather than on Bach's instruments, the clavichord being inaudible a few yards from the player and the harpsichord making long notes evanescent and lacking the dynamic range to mould phrases and make eloquent the ebb and flow of tension'. Robert Dearling admits that his heart often sinks when he reads the legend 'with original instruments', because 'no matter how original the instruments may be, it is the way in which they are played that counts'. Christopher Page is depressed at the title 'Songs for a Tudor King' – 'not another romp through the songs of merrie England with krummhorns and shagbuts?' Fortunately, in this instance, it is otherwise: the music is performed by a vocal quartet.

In the long run, externals count for little: what matters is the presence of early music, which has made a deep impression on many modern composers and has not infrequently surfaced in their works. In many cases this is due to the enthusiasm or persuasion of a scholar, though in others it results from the composer's understandable interest in the meaning and structure of music far distant from our own day and age. There is no reason to believe that Stravinsky was not genuinely moved and inspired by the flamboyant beauty of the manneristic madrigal in his *Monumentum pro Gesualdo*, or that Henze was not insensitive to the Orphic melos of Monteverdi's first dramatic masterpiece in his Sonata for Solo Violin of 1976. Tippett too paid his tribute in the *Preludio al Vespro di Monteverdi* for organ, written in 1946, and doubtless other composers will make their own contributions.

Even a casual glance at the titles of works by Peter

Maxwell Davies will show that he has been influenced to an unusual extent by musical forms of the past. The Wind Sextet is based on Dunstable's motet *Alma Redemptoris Mater*, the Foxtrot for Orchestra on a Pavan by John Bull, and in addition to the opera *Taverner* there are numerous compositions inspired by that once mysterious melange of plainsong and polyphony, the *In nomine*. In more ways than one, Vaughan Williams began a new chapter in English music with his *Fantasia on a Theme of Thomas Tallis*.

Early music of a somewhat later vintage appears in many works of the present century, such as the quotation from Beethoven's Cello Sonata in C, Op. 102, in the middle section of George Rochberg's *Ricordanza*, for cello and piano; and the copious quotations from major composers in Berio's *Sinfonia* or Bernd Alois Zimmermann's *Monologe* (Bach, Beethoven, Debussy, Messiaen). But perhaps the most memorable and beautiful of all such attempts to quote from the classics is Alban Berg's introduction of the chorale 'Es ist genug' from Bach's cantata *O Ewigkeit, du Donnerwort*, in the finale of the Violin Concerto written during the last year of his life.

If the music of the past can thus re-vitalize and fertilize the music of the present, the labours of editors in the cause of early repertoire – whether vocal, instrumental, sacred, secular or occasional — will not have been in vain. In the nature of things, much of what they transcribe belongs to the category of the historical and the antiquarian (for one of the lessons to be learned by early music ensembles is to distinguish between real masterpieces and mere note-spinning), so that in the last resort a choice must be made by a musician rather than a musicologist – unless of course the musicologist is also a musician. And that is a condition greatly to be wished for and highly prized.

Seven
Liturgy and Music

> To understand the theory which underlies
> all things is not sufficient. Theory is but
> the preparation for practice.
> James Stephens: *The Crock of Gold*

Of the serious music known to man over the past thousand years or so, a staggering proportion is directly related to the services of the Christian church through being inspired by or based upon texts in its various languages, and of that proportion by far the greater part is linked to the Catholic liturgy in its various forms. Since Protestant services of whatever kind are relatively straightforward to deal with where music is concerned, problems rarely arise for performers, who need only ascertain what is the correct version before they begin to study and rehearse. It is quite otherwise with Latin church music, for here one is dealing with a lost tradition – a vast and magnificent corpus of chant now rarely sung in churches, many forgotten modes of performance, a dead language, misunderstood liturgical forms, and a long, divergent, and sorrowful history of research that has witnessed (except for the past few years) a blind preoccupation on the part of liturgiologists with liturgy and of musicologists with music. When it was almost too late, they decided to meet and exchange information.

How does all this affect the choir director who may wish to explore the repertoire and present little-known or unknown works to his singers and audience? He may be lucky if he works from recent editions prepared by the still small number of scholars who understand the complex and subtle relationship between liturgy and music. But should he by chance delve further back in time, he can expect to meet with stumbling-blocks of a suspiciously similar pattern no matter what nationality or period of music he chooses to deal with: the very first Kyrie in the Las Huelgas manuscript, a motet by Obrecht, another by Taverner, and a four-part Magnificat by Monteverdi – these range over Spain, the Netherlands, England, Italy; and from the early 14th century to the mid-17th.

All four compositions make use of a classical musico-liturgical device, whereby the different verses or sections are given in strict alternation to a polyphonic group (either solo or choral, depending on the customs and circumstances) and a *schola* whose task it is to perform the plain-song. But the manuscripts and printed editions do not provide the information that our choral director needs to know. Which verse is sung by whom? Where are the missing sections? What can be done to find the texts and music omitted by the scribe or printer? No single book about early music provides the answers to all of these questions, and university courses on music and liturgy are as rare as snow in summer. The principal problems will therefore be summarized and discussed here.

1. *Kyrie 'Rex, virginum amator'*

In Vol. 3 of *El Codex Musical de Las Huelgas* edited by Higini Anglès (Barcelona, 1931) there is a two-part Kyrie on pp. 1-6, with transcriptions of four other Kyries, in smaller type, based on the same chant – No. 4 of the Graduale Romanum. The Kyrie consists of five separate pieces of music, which might fit into a regular alternation pattern in the following manner:

Kyrie (section 1)	2 soloists: 'Rex, virginum amator'
Kyrie	*schola* (chant: lower line of section 1)
Kyrie (section 2)	2 soloists: [untexted]
Christe	*schola* (chant: lower line of section 3)
Christe (section 3)	2 soloists: 'Christe, Dei splendor'
Christe	*schola* (chant: lower line of section 3)

Applied Musicology

Kyrie (section 4)	2 soloists: 'Amborum sacrum'
Kyrie	*schola* (chant: lower line of section 4)
Kyrie (section 5)	2 soloists: [untexted]

This is but one of several possible ways of performance. Once a scheme has been chosen, however, the text (in this case a trope, that is to say the addition of words to an existing melody) should conform to the pattern, but unfortunately the scribe began with one trope ('Rex, virginum') and subsequently passed to another ('Cunctipotens genitor') due to a lapse of memory. The correct text for the *Christe* can be seen (p. 3) in the Wolfenbüttel version. Yet even this is not quite exact according to the alternation scheme – it should be neither 'Christe, Dei splendor' nor 'Christe, Deus de Patre', but 'Quem ventre beato', as may be seen in Wickham Legg's edition of *The Sarum Missal* (Oxford, 1916), p. 5, line 5. (The trope text has often been reprinted, but the source just mentioned is one of the most convenient to consult.) The final problem is the existence of a tenth verse to the Kyrie ('Fac nos post ipsam') and a coda ('Spiritus alme eleyson'); yet this can be solved by underlaying them to the music of the preceding verse.

Ex. 6

102

A reconstruction of this Kyrie, together with a Gloria, Gradual, Sequence, Offertory, Sanctus and Agnus Dei (all from Las Huelgas) can be studied in a performing edition: *Mass in Honour of the Blessed Virgin Mary*, New York Pro Musica Series, No. 22 (G. Schirmer, New York).

2. *Haec Deum Coeli*, by Jacob Obrecht

In Vol. 6 of the collected works of Obrecht, edited by Johannes Wolf (Amsterdam and Leipzig, 1912-1921) a motet *Haec Deum coeli* for five voices appears on pp. 46-48.* The brief critical note on this motet (p. IX) gives no indication of its form and no hint as to the provenance of its text, which is not traceable (as an incipit) in the indices of any missal, antiphoner, processional or other liturgical compilation. Furthermore, it is not traceable in the massive *Index of Gregorian Chant* by John R. Bryden and David G. Hughes (Cambridge, Mass., 1969). Two features of the work nevertheless engage our attention: the use of one of the melodies associated with the hymn *Ut queant laxis*, and a note indicating the festival to which the piece belongs: In Purificatione Mariae. If this 'motet' is in fact a hymn – and since hymn-melodies and texts were traditionally inter-- changeable provided the metres matched – the way to prove it beyond all reasonable doubt is to read the Office for the Purification (February 2) in a breviary, preferably one that dates from the time of Obrecht. It should be noted that the Liber Usualis, on which undue reliance is placed in universities and colleges, ranks merely as a recent compilation of parts of the missal, ritual, gradual, and antiphoner.

*The new Obrecht edition does not so far (1980) include this work.

The hymn given there for Purification is *Ave maris stella*.

An early breviary (or antiphoner, which gives the music in addition to the texts) will provide the necessary background for Obrecht's 'motet'. The Office for the Feast of the Purification, beginning with First Vespers, lists the five psalms and their antiphons, then the responsory *Videte miraculum*, and after this the hymn *Quod chorus vatum* whose second verse is 'Haec Deum coeli' corresponding exactly to Obrecht's 'motet'. In order to perform this work correctly, we should therefore arrange the verses in *alternatim* sequence, beginning with chant, since this was the usual way of performing hymns when a polyphonic choir was available. When it was not, the hymns would still be sung in such a way as to bring about spatial contrast, for the alternation would take place between the two sides of the choir in the north and south stalls. The scheme is therefore as follows:

1. *Schola* (solo): Quod chorus vatum venerandus olim
   Schola (all): Spiritu Sancto cecinit repletus,
   In Dei factum genitrice constat
   Esse Maria.
2. Polyphony: *Haec Deum coeli Dominumque terrae*
3. Schola (all): Quem senex justus Symeon in ulnis . . .
4. Polyphony: *Tu libens votis petimus precantum* . . .
5. Schola (all): Sit Deo nostro decus et potestas . . .

The plainsong for verses 1, 3 and 5 should be transcribed, ideally, from a hymnar of Obrecht's time: the Sarum Antiphoner of 1519 gives a closely-related version. (See Plate 4 on opposite page). Other acceptable versions are found in *Variae preces* (Solesmes, 1901), p. 103; *Hymn Melodies . . . from the Sarum Antiphoner* (London, 1952), p. 17, no. 60; and *Hymnen I*, edited by Bruno Stäblein for *Monumenta Monodica Medii Aevi* (Kassel and Basel, 1956), p. 257, No. 151. It would be even better if the melody were adjusted to conform with Obrecht's cantus firmus, which appears in the Secundus Discantus at the fifth above. As for the polyphony, of which only one verse

Plate 4

Folio 44 of the Proper of Saints, Sarum Antiphoner (1519), showing the hymn *Quod chorus vatum*. The heading 'Purificatio' denotes the feast.

is given, it should obviously carry also the text of verse 4, 'Tu libens votis'. Since in a purely monodic performance both sides of the choir would join in singing the Doxology (verse 5), the polyphonic choir could join with the *schola* for the last verse of the suggested *alternatim* version.

It should be noted that although the *Monumenta Monodica Medii Aevi* represents the best in chant scholarship, it is an extremely difficult book to use without prior experience or knowledge. The hymn melodies are given as they appear in manuscript hymnars of the Middle Ages, each melody being distinctly numbered, and a subscript number added to show each variant. The technique for finding a hymn is to look first in the alphabetical index on p. 663. After each title, the figures in parentheses refer to the volume and page of *Analecta Hymnica* (55 vols., 1886-1922), and the Mel[ody] numbers then refer to the *Gesamtverzeichnis der Melodien* beginning on p. 680. Each melody number is associated with a further set of numbers, of which those in light type may be disregarded since they refer only to the critical report or (when in parentheses) to brief indications. The important numbers are those in heavy type, for these show the pages on which the melodies occur – with the desired text, or with other related texts. Tracing a hymn requires a great deal of patience, but the results can be rewarding.

3. *Audivi*, by John Taverner

In Vol. 3 of *Tudor Church Music* (Oxford, 1924), pp. 35-36 there is a motet by Taverner entitled *Audivi*, set for four high voices – two trebles and two altos. In the introduction to this volume, the liturgical source of the text is identified as Eighth Respond, Matins, All Saints' Day (to which one should add the alternative possibility – First Respond, Matins, Common of Virgins), and if we look up those texts we find that Taverner did not set all of the words to music. He followed one of the two accepted forms of setting responsories by leaving the *schola* section to be sung in plainchant. The form is as follows:

R[espond]: *Audivi* (sung by four soloists)
vocem de caelo venientem: (sung by *schola*)
venite omnes virgines sapientissimae.

r[epetenda]: Oleum recondite in vasis vestris dum
sponsus advenerit.

V[erse]: *Media nocte clamor factus est:* (sung by four soloists)
ecce sponsus venit.

r[epetenda]: Oleum recondite in vasis vestris dum (sung by *schola*)
sponsus advenerit.

The Sarum version of the chant nearest to Taverner's time would be that of the Antiphoner printed in 1519 by F. Byrkman (Pars Hiemalis, *Commune Virginum*, folio xlvii):

Plate 5

Folio 47 [part] Common of Saints, Sarum Antiphoner (1519), showing the responsory *Audivi vocem de caelo*. Heading: 'Commune virginum'.

The chant is used at the same pitch as in the antiphoner, but transposed up to a higher octave, and in order to achieve continuity it is advisable to continue at that octave even though the trebles touch a high B ♭. There was a special reason for this. On All Saint's Day the order of precedence was reversed in singing the nine responsories at Matins, so that instead of beginning with the least important member of the choir and moving upwards, exactly the opposite happened; and by the time the eighth responsory was reached it was the turn of the choirboys. The rubrics state that choirboys, carrying candles, should advance to the altar steps and begin the responsory. Possibly, in the performance that Taverner had in mind, two boys doubled in singing the cantus firmus while the other three took charge of the lower parts. At the word 'Ecce', the boys turn towards the choir, thus confirming the impression that this is a sub-miniature drama in which they, with their high voices, represent the wise virgins (see Matthew 25, 1-6), while the five boys singing the plainchant play the role of the foolish virgins.

This work, and others composed in the same manner and form, ought to be described in programmes not as a motet but as a responsory – its correct liturgical name – and performed accordingly with the proper deployment of solo and choral forces. It should also be noted that the setting by Thomas Tallis, as it appears in the *Historical Anthology of Music*, I, 137 (no. 127) has to be provided with the correct Sarum chant; in addition to which the omitted words 'venite omnes virgines sapientissimae' must be restored, and the section 'Gloria Patri . . . advenit' on p. 138 should be ignored.

4. *Magnificat*, by Monteverdi

A four-voice Magnificat in Vol. 15 (part 2, pp. 703-723) of *Tutte le opere di Claudio Monteverdi* (Asolo, 1940) does not contain the complete text of this well-known canticle. Indeed, even a sidelong glance from a tyro would be sufficient to identify this as an *alternatim* Magnificat; but since the work has been recorded more than once as a solid block of choral polyphony one must assume that it has frequently been mis-performed in that manner, despite the fact that several verses are obviously missing and equally obviously have to be supplied with the correct chant. For absolute authenticity one would have to turn to a Venetian *Tonale* (more specifically one associated with St Mark's) of the first half of the 17th century, but since the formulae for psalms and canticles have changed less than the more elaborate chants of Mass and Office, the versions given in the Roman Antiphoner (or Liber Usualis) may be used. Remember that there is a choice of Simple or Solemn Tones, the latter being reserved for Principal Feasts. They are set forth in the Liber Usualis (edition of 1950) on pp. 207-218, with the Solemn Tones beginning on p. 213.

In this particular case the cantus firmus sections which appear within the polyphonic texture show that Monteverdi had the Simple Tones in mind – see for example the phrase 'ancillae suae' on p. 706 of the score. The even-numbered verses should therefore be sung in chant at the appropriate points, using Tone 1D transposed up a fourth:

Ex. 7

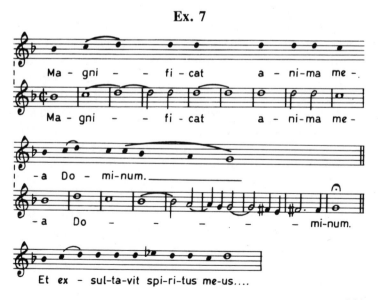

For those who know the liturgy, the foregoing examples will seem over-simplified if not supererogatory; but now that plainsong has become a great rarity as far as its original context is concerned, the indications I have given may serve to guide the interested musician in the direction of further research, should he wish to pursue the matter.

Further Problems of Form

The good editor of today usually, but not always, goes to the trouble of providing the essential monophonic framework for a given polyphonic edifice, so that performers can proceed with the interior decoration. Nevertheless, it will be necessary for several decades to continue using older and less reliable secondary sources, or the extremely old originals which – as has already been pointed out – generally omit the necessary information. Prior to about 1700, everyone guilty of wishing to perform such devilishly complex music was expected to cope at least competently with its inherent vagaries, but this technique became a lost tradition and its re-discovery is less familiar than it should be.

As we have seen in the case of Obrecht, even a simple hymn can sometimes be obscured as far as its form is concerned, due to the practice of composing, copying or printing only the even-numbered verses. 'Adesto nunc propitius', for example, is the second verse of *Salvator mundi Domine*, 'Ignis vibrante lumine' bears the same relationship to *Beata nobis gaudia*, and 'Tu fabricator omnium' to *Jesu salvator saeculi*. A card-index of incipits of second verses is the only perfect solution, yet it is a workable one if the body of hymns to be dealt with is not too large.

Truncated responsories are difficult to deal with as long as they remain unrecognized. In *Tudor Church Music* (Vol. 6, p. 282) a Tallis motet begins 'Quidam fecit cenam magnam', which makes reasonable sense as it stands but needs the intonation 'Homo' to be prefixed in chant, signalling the responsory for First Vespers of Corpus Christi. The same volume also contains (p. 237) a work beginning 'Virtus honor et potestas', but the correct title is 'Honor virtus et potestas' of which the first word must be intoned, as in *Antiphonale Sarisburiense*, pl. 290, where this responsory for Matins of Trinity Sunday appears in full. The music of John Sheppard and other English composers of the time should be examined carefully for this kind of problem.

This principle of integration also holds good for a specialized repertory such as that of Santiago da Compostela, compiled in the latter part of the 12th century. Of the twenty polyphonic items, the two Kyries, Alleluia, Gradual, and four responsories require the addition of chant sections. In his still valuable study, *Die Gesänge der Jakobusliturgie zu Santiago da Compostela* (Freiburg, Switzerland, 1931), Peter Wagner provided all the necessary textual and musical material, but placed it in three different parts of the book, from which it must be patiently re-assembled. In the case of the twelfth responsory, traditionally the most elaborate in form, the information is divided into four. The text of 'O adjutor' (p. 31) demonstrates the basic form, but omits the prosa – which is a trope of the final melisma. 'Portum in ultimo' (the prosa minus music) appears on p. 52, but 'verse 5' is no verse at all: it should read 'ortum' as in the manuscript, since the entire melisma is linked with the word 'portum':

Ex. 8

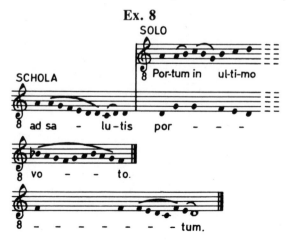

Then on p. 73 we find the chant and text corresponding with p. 31, where the two repeats of 'et duc nos' should of course be completed as far as 'portum'. The prosa begins precisely where the second 'portum' occurs, as may be seen on pp. 119-120. Conductors who enjoy crossword puzzles will find all this to be a challenging alternative and a delightful change, for what results is unquestionably a masterpiece of almost symphonic proportions.

Equally challenging are the English prosa settings, a good example being the *Inviolata* of the Worcester Fragments, in which an unknown composer of the thirteenth century (See Plate 6, opposite page) added harmony of an exquisite tenderness to the final melisma – and its extension – of the responsory for Second Vespers, Feast of the Purification: *Gaude, gaude, gaude Maria*. Only one 'Gaude' was sung when the same responsory occurred at Matins, and this is the version given in the *Antiphonale Sarisburiense*. The fuller version, with prosa, may be seen in a processional (e.g. British Library, Harley 2911), and it is this version that should be linked with *Inviolata*. Whereas the Spanish manuscript referred to above shows a threefold repeat for each line of the prosa, the structure of the Worcester piece hints at the more usual fourfold repeat whereby one melodic phrase would be deployed as follows:

Ex. 9

1. CANTOR: in – vi- o- la – ta in-te-gra et ca-sta es Ma-ri-a,
2. SCHOLA: a ————————————————————————
3. CANTOR: quae es ef-fe-cta ful-gi-da cae-li por-ta,
4. SCHOLA: a ————————————————————————

The rubrics of the breviary direct that the prosa should be performed in this manner, the schola (or choir) remaining seated and responding always on the vowel 'a'.

The polyphonic version, in three-part harmony, carried the chant of each line in the lowest part, but it is broken up

Plate 6

Polyphonic setting of the prose *Inviolata integra* from the so-called
Worcester Fragments (Oxford, Bodleian Library, Lat. liturg. d. 20,
f.23v). Although not easily visible in the facsimile, downward stems have
been added by a later hand, converting the notation in such a way as to
suggest triple metre. In the transcription overleaf, the original notation
has been followed.

by rests and cannot therefore be convincingly underlaid with text. Obviously what happened was that the choral verses sung to the vowel 'a' supported the prosa, which was sung by two soloists:

Ex. 10

A comparable work involving fourfold repetition and the alternation of texted and melismatic tenors is the sequence *Epiphaniam Domino canamus*, in which the verses 'Balaam', 'Et confringet', 'Huic magi' and 'Thure Deum' follow a set pattern, as shown in *The Treasury of English Church Music* (London, 1965), vol. 1, pp. 11-18. Again similar, though on slightly different lines because the responsory carries a double trope within a four-voice harmonic texture is *Januam quam clauserat / Jacinctus in saltibus / Jacet granum*, a fourteenth-century motet in honour of St Thomas of Canterbury. The customary repeat of the latter part of the responsory is followed at once by the prosa 'Clangat pastor in tuba cornea' in which the melodically paired versicles are actually heard four times, since each statement is followed by the melody sung to the vowel 'a'. The overall structure of this work and of the Worcester *Gaude* can best be evaluated in performance, or on available records (Nonesuch H-71292 and H-71308).

An exceptionally clear and useful exposition of the prose is given in Frank Harrison's *Music in Medieval Britain* (London, 1958), pp. 67-70, where he points out that the term prosa was used in France as a synonym for sequence. Indeed they shared certainly similarities of form, notably the paired verses, and as the one was an offshoot of the responsory, the other followed the Alleluia. In the absence of specific rubrics on the singing of sequences, it is possible that in some cases each verse was immediately followed by a melismatic (untexted) version of the theme, as in the tenor part of *Epiphaniam* referred to above and in the two proses. But even if this is not done, at least the two verses for each theme should be sung in full, since the principle of repetition is inherent in the structure of the sequence. Yet from time to time this is forgotten, as in the Spanish recordings of three sequences from *La Música a Catalunya fins al segle XIII*, by Higini Anglés (Barcelona, 1935).

Cantantibus hodie, Alleluia: persona nostra iocunda, and *Potestati magni* are all performed as if the sequence form had never existed, for all we hear is verses 1a, 2a, 3a, and so forth. In the case of *Potestati magni*, the inevitable old instruments play each verse before the text is heard, and even when we do hear it, voices sing only the lower part, instruments again appearing on the upper part. Exceptionally, the prose for *Viri galilei: In eadem quippe* is correctly performed; but the succeeding *Hosanna: Sospitati dedit mundum* loses the even-numbered verses again, though the music is repeated in each case by instruments. All these examples, of course, destroy not only the form of the sequence but the sense of the poetry. Some idea of the result can be gathered from an attempt to recite your favourite poem while leaving out alternate lines.

Finally, a word of warning about texts, and especially about hurried attempts to identify liturgical occasions by means of incipits. The usual index, giving the first few words of a chant or composition, can prove a snare and a pitfall to those unwary amateurs who imagine that this kind of basic research is an easy matter. Basic it may be, but it is not always easy. Here are some examples, beginning with a motet by Lionel Power, *Salve sancta parens*, in *Corpus mensurabilis musicae* 50, vol. 1. The critical notes inform us that we are dealing with the 'introit, at mass, BVM?', and it is true that the standard introit for Lady Masses from Candlemas to Advent was, with few exceptions, *Salve sancta parens enixa puerpera regem*; but Power's text diverges after the first three words continuing 'speciosa Regina polorum'. The subsequent end-rhymes 'miserorum' and 'saeculorum' indicate that this is more likely to be a hymn or part of a rhymed office, but probably not an introit.

In the edition of Giaches de Wert's five-voice motets of 1566 (*Corpus mensurabilis musicae* 24, vol. 11), *Domine, si tu es* is described as part of the Mass, Octave Day of SS Peter and Paul, Apostles. The only occurrence of this text on this particular day is in the middle of the Gospel, but because the text diverges from what de Wert has set to music, it cannot be classified as a setting of a complete Gospel as is no. 16 in the collection, *Intravit Jesus* – for the feast of the Assumption, BVM (and not, as the notes tell us, 'relegated to minor feast days'). The point about *Domine, si tu es* is that it comes not from the Mass but from the Office, specifically from the eighth responsory for Matins of SS Peter and Paul, June 29. A much more puzzling attempt at identification calls *Transeunte Domino* (no. 8) a 'Sequence for Quinquagesima Sunday at Mass; *cf.*

Antiphon, Transeunte Domino'. One first wonders what a sequence has to do with an antiphon, until a casual reference to that most dangerously edged of tools, the Liber Usualis, reveals that 'sequentia sancti Evangelii secundum Lucam' ('continuation of the Gospel according to St Luke') has been misinterpreted as 'sequence' in the sense of a liturgical poem set to music. In any event, the Gospel in question does not correspond with the text set by de Wert, though it does have some affinity with an antiphon at Terce:

Gospel:	————————————————
Antiphon:	Transeunte Domino, clamabat caecus ad eum:
Motet:	Transeunte Domino, clamabat caecus ad eum,

G:	et qui praeibant, increpabant eum ut taceret Ipse
A:	————————————————— ——
M:	et qui praeibant, increpabant eum. ————Ipse

G:	vero multo magis clamabat: Fili David, miserere mei.
A:	———————————————— miserere mei,
M:	vero multo magis clamabat: ———— miserere mei,

G:	————
A:	Fili David.
M:	Fili David.

Giovanni Gabrieli's motets have sometimes suffered sadly from mis-interpretation; and if their skilled advocates plead erroneously, how can the choral conductor explain the latent meaning and emotion of the music to his keen but baffled forces? *Benedicam Dominum* has nothing to do with the Fifth Sunday after Pentecost, although the offertory for that day begins with the same two words – and thereafter diverges. *Judica me Domine* sets the first five verses of Psalm 25 for double choir, and therefore has nothing to do with Passion Sunday, whose introit begins *Judica me Deus* (from Psalm 42). *Quis es iste qui venit de Edom*, another double choir motet from the *Sacrae Symphoniae* of 1597, certainly coincides (as far as the first few words are concerned) with the vespers anti-phon, Feast of the Most Precious Blood, but it cannot possibly relate to that feast since its extended text is punc-tuated by joyous Alleluias, in tripla. The text as a whole shows that Gabrieli is dealing with a Christmas piece, of which the next motet in the collection – *Hodie Christus natus est* – is the second half. Both halves share the same mode, identical voice-part designations (C A 5 8 T / 7 9 10 6 B), and an obviously matching design. Another splendid Christmas motet has rarely if ever been recognized as such for the simple reason that scholars are so busy 'analysing' the music that the text passes by unnoticed and unread; yet *Audite principes* deserves an honoured place alongside *Quem vidistis, pastores* and *Angelus ad pastores ait.*

The moral of this matter is that snap judgments do no good to the reputation of the judge and only serve to confound the readers or listeners. Either the study of music and liturgy must be taken seriously, or the matter must be referred to experts in the field. If musicology is to be considered more and more as a truly scientific branch of an essentially humanistic and artistic discipline, the care and accuracy normally associated with scientific research should be lavished on music too. Anything less than this is inadequate; and inadequacy is no hall-mark of true musi-cianship.

Eight

Ornamentation

> Good embellishments must be distin-
> guished from bad, the good must be
> correctly performed, and introduced
> moderately and fittingly.
>
> C. P. E. Bach: *Essay on the True Art of
> Playing Keyboard Instruments*

If it is true that each man kills the thing he loves, ornamentation in music has quite frequently been done to death, not
only in past centuries when it was a recognized part of what
might be described as a melismatic sub-culture, but in even
more recent times when early music has been much revived
and too often over-restored. As more and more examples
of ornamentation come to light, either in treatises or in
manuscripts and printed editions of repertoire prior to the
present century, the matter and manner of its deployment
present an increasing number of problems, the solution of
which is not nearly as slick and smooth a business as some
prefer to think.

The ability to choose and use ornamentation with some
degree of success in modern performances of early music
may indeed be acquired by reading textbooks and treatises,
but in the long run it is a question not of great knowledge
but of good taste, which depends on intuition rather than
acquisition. The lack of good taste has from time
immemorial brought forth the thunder of critics and
musicians, whose reactions have been prompted by the
gilding not only of lilies but of all the flowers in Euterpe's
chaplet. Nothing has been spared – solo song, church
music, opera, keyboard music, oratorio, instrumental

compositions of all types. What began in monody could obviously be pursued in polyphony.

As early as 1142, when Ailred of Rievaulx wrote his *Speculum caritatis*, the gentle art of embellishment (possibly also improvised harmonization) was gnawing at the very foundations of monastic worship:

> To what purpose serves that contraction and inflection of the voyce? This man sings a base, this a small meane, another a treble, a fourth divides and cuts asunder, as it were, certain middle notes. One while the voyce is strained, anon it is remitted, now it is dashed, and then againe it is inlarged with a lowder sound. Sometimes, which is a shame to speak, it is enforced into a horse's neighings; sometimes, the masculine vigour being laid aside, it is sharpened into the shrillnesse of a woman's voyce; now and then it is writhed, and retorted with a certain artificiall circumvolution. (*Translated by William Prynne, 1600-69*)

In John of Salisbury's *Policraticus*, written in 1159 and dedicated to Thomas Becket, then archdeacon of Canterbury, we find sharply barbed criticisms of singers, both in regard to their foppish and feministic type of tone-production (an attack on counter-tenors?), and their fondness for running up and down the scale (*tirade* or *course* in the vocabulary of 17th century France), or for cutting notes apart and joining them again (surely a reference to hocket). A century later, the *Statuta antiqua* of the Carthusian Order deplore singers who break up notes, repeat them, and indulge in waves of ornamentation.

Further fulminations in the early 14th century show that long-established opposition had done little to correct the excesses of those insufferable virtuosi. Jacques de Liège, in his *Speculum musicae*, spoke of singers lacking good style who descant too wantonly and multiply superfluous notes, while Pope John XXII issued a decree aimed at polyphony in general which accuses choir singers of truncating melodies with hockets, depraving them with descants, and allowing their voices to run to and fro, intoxicating the ear rather than soothing it. Examples of this outrageous passage-work loom large in medieval music from the earliest times, for much of it was not only sung but actually written down. Some of it sounds tame nowadays, and if the following is an example of ordinary embellishment, the downright florid ought not to have proved too shocking. The plain version is from Oxford, Bodleian Library, Arch. Selden, B.14, f.312 (col. 1); the coloured one from British Library, Sloane MS. 1210, f. 139. Both are from the mid-14th century:

Ex. 11

What is the performer to do, faced as he might well be with the prospect of adding ornamentation to a vocal or instrumental line in the style of a given period? In this, true authenticity must yield to intelligent guesswork, but even that can only be put into operation when certain guidelines have been thoroughly understood and accepted. The first is to narrow down the ornamental style to the approximate date and place of the original, so that if you are dealing with Rameau, look up the book by his friend Jean Baptiste Bérard, *L'Art du chant*, dedicated to Mme de Pompadour in 1755. There you will find an air from Rameau's *Castor et Pollux* with Bérard's annotations, which can be expanded into a 'performing edition' as Jane Arger has done in her excellent but little-known *Les Agréments et Le Rhythme* (Paris, 1918):

Ex. 12

Bérard's realization of the ornaments:

Rameau's text annotated by Bérard:

Tris - tes ap-prêts,

pâ - les flam-beaux, Jour plus af-freux que les té-

- ne - bres, As - tres lu - gu - bres des tom-beaux,

The second guideline, of no less importance, is to accept the spirit rather than the substance of what is given – for a lack of taste is not peculiar to any one epoch. In other words, less is usually better than more, and the small makes a greater impact than the large. For ornamentation is essentially a miniature art, a by-product of music, and it should never be made to appear fundamental. It is an offshoot and an excrescence — it should be held in check and treated with care.

Examples of Ornamentation

It goes without saying that the literature on ornamentation is vast, and grows greater from year to year. The best reference work in English is Robert Donington's *The Interpretation of Early Music*, which is continually being kept up-to-date in new editions. Also recommended are Hans-Peter Schmitz, *Die Kunst der Verzierung im 18. Jahrhundert* (Cassel and Basel, 1955) and Ernst T. Ferand, *Improvisation in Nine Centuries of Western Music* (Cologne, 1961), both valuable for their many complete musical examples. Another useful book is Howard M. Brown's *Embellishing Sixteenth Century Music* (London, 1976). For an admirable summary in German, Georg von

Dadelsen's article ('Verzierung') in *Die Musik in Geschichte und Gegenwart* is a model of its kind. Recorded illustrations may be found in *The Art of Ornamentation*, Vanguard Records, HM 47-48 SD. But there is no single book that covers the development of the art from the Middle Ages to the present, so that in its absence one can only fill in the gaps gradually from specialized publications.

The earliest large-scale source of information, interestingly enough, is not a treatise but a 14th-century manuscript probably copied at Ferrara but now in Faenza, whence its name 'The Faenza Codex'. It has been exhaustively studied by Dragan Plamenac, whose splendid edition *Keyboard Music of the Late Middle Ages in the Faenza Codex 117* is published by the American Institute of Musicology. The title may be somewhat restrictive, for while there are undoubtedly many pieces that might have been intended for early keyboard instruments, the incidence of cadences on a unison (which would be 'lost' on an instrument such as the organetto that Landini plays in the well-known Squarcialupi portrait) suggests that many of the arrangements could be examples of the duo or *bicinium*. The following extract from the madrigal *Non al suo amante* by Jacopo da Bologna shows how the upper voice-part is delicately embellished while the lower remains substantially as in the original. The ease with which original and decorated lines can be compared is one of the main features of this edition:

Ex. 13

There is one important rule that must be observed when adding ornamentation, no matter what the nationality or period: all new material should make good harmony and (if necessary) convincing counterpoint with the supporting parts or voices. The early treatises, however, leave such subtleties to the interpreter, who is supposed to know how to deal with difficult situations such as might arise in applying the more florid *passaggi* in *La Fontegara* (Venice, 1535), named after the village where its author, Sylvestro de Ganassi, was born. Primarily a tutor for the flute, this useful little book also offers assistance in 'diminution', as the art of ornamentation was sometimes called. Each interval, ascending and descending, is provided with a number of appropriate melodic figures, at first slow and then in smaller and quicker notes. In the *Regola Terza*, one of the formulae for a descending fifth (G to C) is embellished more and more until the original descending figure

125

begins to proceed rapidly in the opposite direction. Both would make reasonable sense in a conjectural harmonic framework:

Ex. 14

It will doubtless be noted that although the more florid version moves dutifully from *g* to *d* (as does the simpler one) it creates passing dissonances and a pair of consecutive fifths, which brings to mind Juan Bermudo's strictures on ornament-happy keyboard players in his *Declaración de instrumentos musicales* (Ossuna, 1555). In the Fourth Book, Chapter 43, he complains that very few players are willing and able to ornament as fluently with their left hand as with their right. As for tenor parts, taken by stiff fingers and thumb . . .! Then come the consecutive fifths and octaves, *fa* against *mi* where it is not allowed, dissonances galore, and even strange consonances. Nicola Vicentino, whose *L'Antica musica ridotta alla moderna prattica* also appeared in 1555 (Antonio Barre, Rome), considers ornamentation more effective in five-part harmony than in four-part, since there is more chance of sustained harmony should the diminution pass by a crucial note too quickly. In another passage he recommends heterophony as a solution, with instruments sustaining the polyphonic web while only the voices are permitted to ornament.*

---

* The degree of confusion that sometimes plagues scholars both ancient and modern may be sensed when looking for this passage in the original publication, or in a facsimile of it. Sometimes the reference is given simply as 'chapter 42'

Zarlino, in his *Istitutioni harmoniche* (Venice, 1558) reveals that he dwelt among embellishment fiends – though this was well before the heyday of Bassano, Conforto, Rogniono, and Bovicelli – and he launches a bitter attack on them in the latter half of Part III, Chapter 46. Especially blameworthy are the musicians who make a pretence of skill and knowledge by introducing ornaments so wild and so outrageous that not only are the listeners fatigued – the music is ruined by wrong harmonies and faulty partwriting. Apparently these things were ordered better in France, for little is said about ornamentation in the 16th century, apart from a remark in Anthoine de Bertrand's preface to the *Premier livre des Amours de Ronsard* of 1578, where it is said to confuse the harmony and make a sad composition sound happy.

On the other hand, vocal embellishment often seems to have been associated with style and sweetness, as in a letter from Andrea Calmo to the Venetian courtesan Signora Calandra, written about 1550:

> As for your singing, I have never heard better: what a beautiful voice, what style, what runs and divisions, what sweetness – enough to soften the cruellest, hardest, wickedest heart in the world!

The power and persuasiveness of a singer who had mastered the art must have been apparent to all those who read a lengthy letter by Giovanni Camillo Maffei, a medical doctor who lived in Solofra, not far from Naples. Writing to his friend the Count of Altavilla, Maffei tried to sum up the art of singing as it was then understood, together with a few examples of ornamented cadences for different vocal ranges and a list of five basic rules. Although the letter was

without mentioning the fact that one must first know which book ('Libro') each one numbering the chapter afresh. Sometimes the only reference is 'page 88', but the volume is foliated, not paginated, and the first f. 88 does not contain the passage in question. The second f. 88 – actually a misprint for 94 – contains the 'Regola da concertare concertando ogni sorte di compositione'. Vicentino does not improve the situation, for his index to Libro Quarto refers the reader to f. 92, chapter 43!

published at Naples in 1562, it was not carefully discussed and illustrated until recently, when Nanie Bridgman wrote her article 'G.C. Maffei et sa lettre sur le chant', *Revue de Musicologie* XXXVIII (1956), 3-34.

The German writer Hermann Finck, in his *Musica Practica* (Wittenberg, 1556), criticizes those self-taught musicians

> who manage somehow to sing without the aid of a teacher, and do not hesitate to make use of organ ornaments, which are quite incorrect in a vocal context because some of them tear good music to bits, in the same way that puppies chew people's clothes.

He adds that ornaments should be used sparingly, and only occasionally are two parts ornamented at the same time. Francisco Guerrero, laying down guidelines for instrumental ornamentation at Seville in 1586, cannot countenance simultaneous glossing, as Robert Stevenson has shown in his formidable study of *Spanish Cathedral Music in the Golden Age* (Berkeley and Los Angeles, 1961), p. 167:

> First, Rojas and López shall always play the treble parts: ordinarily on shawms. They must carefully observe some order when they improvise glosses, both as to places and to times. When the one player adds glosses to his part, the other must yield to him and play simply the written notes; for when both together gloss at the same time, they produce absurdities that stop one's ears. Second, the same Rojas and López when they at appropriate moments play on cornetts must again each observe the same moderation in glossing: the one deferring to the other because, as has been previously said, for both simultaneously to add improvised glosses creates insufferable dissonance. As for Juan de Medina, he shall ordinarily play the contralto part, not obscuring the trebles nor disturbing them by exceeding the glosses that belong to a contralto. When on the other hand his part becomes the top above the sackbuts, then he is

left an open field in which to glory and is free to add all the glosses that he desires and knows so well how to execute on his instrument.

Although many books on ornamentation were published in Italy in the 16th century, one in particular deserves to be singled out for its neat and concise organization – Giovanni Luca Conforto's *Breve et facile maniera d'essercitarsi* (Rome, 1593), re-issued in facsimile as no. 2 in *Veröffentlichungen der Musik-Bibliothek Paul Hirsch* (Berlin, 1922). Conforto, who spent most of his life in Rome, also sang at the court of Ferrara, and was widely known through his publications. Vincenzo Giustiniani found his singing too florid, but those who heard him in his famous series of Lenten concerts given in Rome during the latter part of the 16th century commented enthusiastically on his improvisation and virtuosity. His little book amply demonstrates his mastery of ornamentation, and since it ranges from the very simple to the extremely effusive the modern practitioner has much from which to choose.

The lengthy title tells us that instrumentalists as well as singers can make good use of the exercises, which begin with a two-note ascending cadence ('Salve') preceded by a series of seven clefs, showing that the examples can begin on any note of the scale, and at any pitch:

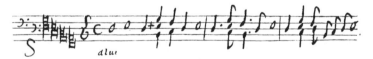

The 'variations on two notes' become more florid and fanciful as they proceed, and very often they are provided with alternate routes to fit different harmonic contexts. Taking the first example (marked with a small cross by Conforto to show that it is one of three recommended variations in the set), we find the following best possibilities, suitable for various harmonizations of which those given are of course capable of modification. The whole idea of the book is flexibility:

Ex. 15

The next figure (p. 5, 'Mater') is extremely useful because it consists of a two-note descending cadence, which is of very frequent occurrence in songs and arias, also in works for the stage:

Ex. 16(a)

In the course of editing Monteverdi's *Il Ballo delle Ingrate* (Schott, 1960), I found so many examples of this favourite 'tenor cadence' that it seemed more than appropriate to borrow some of Conforto's configurations in order to relieve the tedium; and it is reasonably certain that the composer – who was under considerable emotional and physical strain at the time – refrained from writing in the ornaments since he trained the soloists to display their *gorgie* as best they knew.* The point was to persuade the singers to make the embellishments sound completely natural and extemporized. As Jacopo Peri wrote of Vittoria Archilei in the preface to his *Eurydice* (1601):

> This lady, who has always made my compositions seem worthy of her singing, adorns them not only with these trills and these long vocal embellishments, simple and double,† which her lively imagination can invent at any moment (more to comply with the usage of our times than because she considers the beauty and strength of our singing to lie in them) but also with those – both lovely and charming – that cannot be written, or if written, cannot be learned from writing.

Here are two examples of the way in which Conforto's figures can be adapted to fit perfectly with Monteverdi's cadences:

Ex. 16(b, c)

* An amusing example of how not to do this came to my notice shortly after the Schott edition was published. A recording of *Il Ballo delle Ingrate* followed the text of the edition with regard to the places at which I had suggested ornamentation. But the conductor, anxious to avoid paying copyright fees, used only the first half of each flourish as printed, changing the cadences in such a manner as to make them 'original'. The soloists, as far as I can recall, sounded very confused indeed.

† For examples of 'simple' and 'double' embellishments, see Ex. 20, p. 136.

Applied Musicology

Conforto gives equally variegated examples for ascending and descending thirds, fourths and fifths, then come unisons and octaves followed by a veritable treasure-house of myriapodic melismata, leading at last to a highly important section dealing with the various kinds of *groppo* – our trill, more or less – and the original *trillo*, which was not far removed from a glottal vibrato, sometimes static, sometimes mobile. (See Plate 7 opposite).

The *trillo*, which Giovanni Battista Doni called 'a rippling (*increspamento*) or vibration of the voice', is a useful and effective ornament appearing in two distinct guises, related to each other through the manner of production. Giulio Caccini, in his famous song collection of 1602, *Le Nuove Musiche*, explains them in clear if perhaps over-simplified music examples: one is long and based on a single pitch, while the other is shorter and descends through a major or minor third:

Ex. 17(a, b)

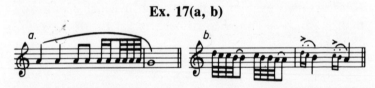

In actual practice the rhythmic notation given by Caccini was released from its straight-jacket so that the quickening-up seemed gradual rather than contrived as in 17a; and as for 17b, it probably sounded as in the next bar, with the glottal effect binding and separating the notes simultaneously. Further fascinating details about this ornament are discussed in Carol MacClintock's article 'Caccini's *Trillo* – a Re-examination', *Bulletin of the National Association of Teachers of Singing* XXXIII (1976), 38-44.

Another special effect was the *ribattuto della gola*, in which a series of short upper auxiliary notes 'beat' against the principal note. There is a fine example of this (followed closely by a written-out *trillo*) in Monteverdi's *Combattimento di Tancredi e Clorinda*, where the partbook for the

Plate 7

Ornamentation patterns from Conforto: *Breve et facile maniera* (1593).

continuo shows only the simple form as opposed to the tenor solo partbook carrying the ornaments in full:

Ex. 18

Later periods of ornamentation, extremely well documented in the books by Brown, Donington, Ferand and Schmitz listed earlier, are much easier to comprehend especially since there are so many models to follow, including several that demonstrate how a composer would set about ornamenting one of his own works. A particularly beautiful example from J.S. Bach is his transformation of a sinfonia into the slow movement of a concerto. The introductory movement of the Cantata No. 156 ('Ich steh' mit einem Fuss im Grabe') is set out for solo oboe and strings, marked 'Adagio', as a smoothly-shaped cantilena almost without any' decoration whatever (Bach Gesellschaft, XXXII, p. 99). But when Bach drew upon his melody for the Largo of his Harpsichord Concerto in F minor (B.G. XVII, p. 142), he embellished the solo line with the object not so much of giving the soloist the opportunity to show off his skill, as of helping him sustain the evanescent tones of his instrument:

Ex. 19(a, b)

If French taste was not so strongly directed towards ornamentation in earlier periods, it made up for it in the 18th century, when we find Handel's friend Mrs Mary Delaney writing (on 10 December 1750) to a friend about a forthcoming rehearsal of *Messiah* in Dublin, which Giovanni Battista Morella was to conduct. Despite his name, Morella leaned towards the French fashion in cadential flourishes:

> I am afraid *his French taste* will prevail; I shall *not be able to endure* his introducing *froth and nonsense* in that sublime and awful piece of music. What makes me fear this will be the case, is, that in the closing of the eighth concerto of Corelli, instead of playing it *clear and distinct*, he filled it up with *frippery and graces which quite destroyed the effect* of the sweet notes, and solemn pauses that conclude it.

Some twenty years prior to this, the same lady witnessed the triumph of *The Beggar's Opera* over the Italian operas then being given in London, yet the one went the way of the other as far as ornamentation was concerned – and we have Dr Burney's word for it:

135

But either from the ambition of the singer, or expectations of the audience, Music is not suffered to remain simple long upon the stage; and the more plain and ancient the melodies, the more they are to be embellished by every new performer of them. The tunes in *The Beggar's Opera* will never appear in their original simple garb again.

In Italy, which seems to have been the cradle of it all, ornamentation techniques were being carried over industriously from one generation to the next. Pier Francesco Tosi's much translated *Opinioni de' cantori antichi e moderni* (Bologna, 1723) makes it clear that composers are not expected to write ornaments into the score, and he is followed in this by the *Riflessioni pratiche sul canto figurato* (Milan, 1777) of Giovanni Battista Mancini. Mancini, like Peri before him, believed that singers could not successfully learn the art of embellishment from written-out examples, and accordingly gives only a few specimens of the *volatina*:

Ex. 20

volatina semplice

volatina raddoppiata

Further information about Mancini and his contemporaries, in particular Lorenzoni and Galeazzi, may be found in a short but very useful study by Joan E. Smiles, 'Directions for Improvised Ornamentation in Italian Method Books of the Late Eighteenth Century', *Journal of the American Musicological Society* XXXI (1978), 495-509.

Studying in Milan in 1838, the English singer Clara Novello took it into her head to write to Rossini on the question of ornamentation in a *cabaletta*, and his answer was brief and to the point:

The repeat is made expressly that each singer may vary it, so as best to display his or her peculiar capacities: therefore the first time the composer's music should be exactly given.

Having been involved in a personality struggle with the castrato Velluti at rehearsals of *Aureliano in Palmira* in 1814, Rossini had vowed that in future he would write out all of his own *fioriture* and make the singers perform them, which Velluti had refused to do. Accordingly he wrote out several for Clara Novello, but their present whereabouts appears to be unknown.

Other repositories of embellishment in 19th century opera have fared somewhat better. Possibly the most complete and remarkable of these is the collection of one printed book and seven manuscript notebooks formerly the property of Mme Cinti-Damoreau (1801-63), who compiled them during the course of her long and distinguished career as a singer at the Paris Opéra and the Théâtre Italien, where she worked closely with Rossini. With her voice in mind he wrote all the leading female roles of his Paris operas, excerpts from which are copied into her books alongside ornamented passages from operas by Halévy, Bellini, Meyerbeer, Donizetti, Auber, Isouard, Boieldieu and many others. The volumes in question are now in the Lilly Library of Indiana University, and an account of them is given in Austin Caswell's fascinating article 'Mme Cinti-Damoreau and the Embellishment of Italian Opera in Paris: 1820-45', *Journal of the American Musicological Society* XXVIII (1975), 459-492. The following excerpt shows two of Cinti-Damoreau's cadential flourishes for the aria 'Come per me sereno' in Bellini's *La Sonnambula.*(See Ex. 21, p.138).

Earl Rogers, in his invaluable study of 'Ecco ridente' (from Rossini's *Il Barbiere di Siviglia*) in the same periodical that contains the article on Caccini's *trillo* (see p.132) makes the point that much can be learned from early recorded performances, specifically those by Fernando de Lucia (1860-1925), Edmond Clément (1867-1928), Tito

Ex. 21

Schipa (1889-1965) and Richard Conrad. The following excerpt – bars 17-19 – displays the remarkable divergence of ideas and approaches in a single cadence:

Ex. 22

Undoubtedly things sometimes went too far, as Mendelssohn so often hints in his correspondence. He noticed with faint amusement that the Papal Choir sang unique versions of Palestrina motets in which embellishments had been added to all the voice-parts without exception, occasionally producing very strange effects. On the other hand he was captivated by the *Miserere* of Allegri, 'a simple series of chords on which ornaments have been superimposed. . . . These always recur on the same chords, and as they are cleverly devised and beautifully adapted to the voice, one always enjoys hearing hem'. (Letter of 4 April 1831.) Although one assumes that so able a musician would write down what he heard with a high degree of accuracy, especially the single line of unison chant, it is not easy to reconcile his reported version of the responsory *Tenebrae factae sunt* (letter of 16 June 1831 to C.F. Zelter) with that in the modern chant books. Perhaps the Papal Choir took the same kind of liberty in monophony as they did in polyphony. Mendelssohn's caustic comments on Roman orchestral players include a remark to the effect that the woodwind players execute flourishes like those usually heard in farmyards. Perhaps some of the musicians still possessed tattered copies of Conforto. On the whole, however, it seems not to have been much worse than Munich, where he heard a performance of *Fidelio* in which the singer entrusted with the role of Marzelline introduced all sorts of flourishes into her part.

Whatever could be done to Beethoven could certainly be inflicted upon Mozart, as is clear from an account given by Hector Berlioz to the historian Taine about a performance of *Figaro* at Drury Lane Theatre, London, on 11 February 1848. Berlioz was determined to conduct the work exactly in accordance with the score, nothing to be added, nothing taken away. But when he came to rehearse 'Voi che sapete' the lady singing Cherubino introduced all manner of fioriture. 'Mademoiselle', said Berlioz with icy politeness, 'is it your music master who has pencilled in these embellishments for your song?' She admitted as much, and Berlioz continued: 'Well, tell him from me that he's a fool. You will sing the song as it is, or we shall not accompany you'.

In 1905 George Bernard Shaw went to Covent Garden for a performance of *Don Giovanni*, and wrote one of his sprightliest letters to *The Times* shortly afterwards denouncing the then current fashion for outrageous headgear, more especially since the lady sitting directly in front of him and obscuring (one would imagine) his line of sight 'had stuck over her right ear the pitiable corpse of a large white bird'; and as if this were not enough he was obliged to listen to various 'improvements on Mozart' by Signor Caruso. The entire letter, which is well worth reading, can be found reprinted in *The First Cuckoo: Letters to The Times since 1900* (London, 1976), 56-58.

Now that the art of embellishment has been revived on a grand and scholarly scale, it has become accessible to more and more performers thanks to reprints of sources. Yet the basic problems remain the same as in former times: used to excess, any ornament in any walk of life can in the long run prove obnoxious, and this is also true of music. It is therefore up to the performer and his sense of good taste to make sure that his audiences are not stunned or nauseated, but rather beguiled by the art whose true success lies in hiding art, and in the end impressed by the qualities of restraint and fine judgement.

In Colley Cibber's *Apology* (1740) there is an anecdote about Purcell and one of his choristers, which (whether it be true or not) gently hints that a properly developed natural gift is worth far more than something artificially contrived:

> [Jemmy Bowen], when practising a Song set by Mr Purcell, some of the Musicians told him to grace and run a Division in such a Place. 'O, let him alone!' said Mr Purcell, 'he will grace it more naturally than you, or I, can teach him'.

Nine
Instrumentation

> At the *Salve Regina*, one of the three ver-
> ses that are played shall be on shawms,
> one on cornetts, and the other on record-
> ers; because always hearing the same
> instrument annoys the listener.
>
> Francisco Guerrero (1586)

Although the art of orchestration existed in many forms
and on many levels long before Berlioz wrote his *Grand
Traité* in 1844, codifying and collecting all the information
available to him at that time, it was never a subject that
appealed to theorists. One can search diligently through
the medieval treatises published by Gerbert and Cous-
semaker without finding more than passing references to
instruments, although documents, diaries, letters, and all
manner of pictorial presentations demonstrate that large
numbers of instruments were in daily use in the home, at
court, and sometimes in church. Since their musical role
was never defined in early sources as, for instance, the role
of strings, woodwind, brass and percussion is defined in
scores and sets of parts issued from 1600 onwards, the
entire field of the Middle Ages and the Renaissance has
become once more a happy hunting-ground for amateur
orchestrators. And that is precisely the way it should be.
The aleatory principle was all-pervasive in those centuries
that resisted, perhaps for good reason, any kind of slavish
adherence to a prototype. An unpredictable though not
unplanned change of timbre was often welcome (as Guerrero hinted in his instructions, quoted above, to the
instrumentalists at Seville Cathedral) but its exact nature
depended upon the resources available.

Medieval and Renaissance Music

Over the past half-century or so, the instrumentation of medieval music has undergone a bewildering variety of changes. Most of these can be more or less justified by reiterating the age-old plea 'We don't know exactly what they did in the Middle Ages' – 'they' being the practitioners whose unenviable task it was to impress order and discipline upon picturesque pickup groups as illustrated in illuminated manuscripts. The obvious reply, of course, is 'But we do know exactly what they didn't do'. One thing I am sure they didn't do was to add drums, nackers, and other percussion instruments to everything in sight, whether or not its character might seem to call for such a boisterous display of good spirits, yet such is the current fashion in modern records of ancient music that the novice might be forgiven for assuming that time was never again beaten with such persistently rhythmic ferocity as it was in the days of William the Conqueror.

During the highly concentrated course of the Beethoven Festival held in Vienna in 1927, one particularly remarkable event captured the ears and the imaginations of many who must have attended out of sheer curiosity. It was a concert of medieval music organized by an eminent scholar, Rudolf von Ficker, then newly appointed to the chair of musicology at Vienna University. Based on his own transcriptions of music from Pérotin to Dunstable, the performing editions used for that memorable concert were also his, as was the work of rehearsing and conducting the vocal and instrumental forces. Considering the fact that modern instruments were consistently used (and with good effect), and bearing in mind the occasional reversals of roles – in Pérotin's *Sederunt principes* the solo parts were sung by chorus and vice-versa – the overall impression received by the majority of listeners was one of wonderment and rapture. A new door had been opened onto the past.

Practical suggestions

Be aware of, but at the same time beware of ephemeral fads and fashions. Filiation, water-marks, computerization and iconography can be good tools or bad masters. Iconography, for example, proves nothing whatever in regard to the use of instruments in earlier times. It can only show what the artist, whoever or wherever he might have been, may or may not have seen at an unknown point in time. Not even a recurring pattern can be accepted as proof absolute that such and such a combination of instruments was generally or undeniably put together for a given occasion, for artists (like musicians) tended to copy each other. On the other hand, a complex of evidences constructed from prose and poetry, sources and resources, miniatures and manuscripts may cautiously be admitted to point to the possibility of certain practices, though even then there is no substitute for the 'feel' of the situation – something that can only come from long and varied experience.

Organum, to give but one example, is extremely difficult to bring off because so much depends upon matters of internal balance and acoustics. The music must be clear, not mushy; and if instruments are used to double the voices there should be no imbalance. Much can be gleaned from a small book published in 1958 but largely ignored and never translated: Walter Krüger's *Die authentische Klangform des primitiven Organum* (Kassel and Basel). He points out that since the writings of the Church Fathers frequently stress the undesirability of using instruments in church, the practice may have been fairly common. On the other hand, some sources admit that instruments can be used in alternating forms such as psalms and sequences. The practice of heterophony, whereby voices and instruments perform the same basic material yet with certain differences (pitch, figuration) related to their individual characteristics, is touched upon with reference to non-western as well as western music.

Also of great interest is a contribution by Gilbert Reaney to *Aspects of Medieval and Renaissance Music* (New York,

1966), 705-722 – 'The Performance of Medieval Music'. It is stated there that while the organ might have supported, with its long held notes, the more rapidly-moving upper parts in an organum by Pérotin, it would also have been possible to supply a vocal drone bass by means of 'staggered' breathing. Yet at a slightly later period – the 14th century – untexted parts are usually assumed to be instrumental. Our attention is also drawn to a Veronese picture-book of that time, showing three musicians, one of them singing while the other two play on the portative organ and a viol. The caption *organum cantare vel sonare* could mean 'to harmonize a song' or 'to accompany a song on the organ and viol'. Professor Reaney considers that the organ could have been playing heterophony with the voice, ornamenting its line to a suitable degree; though the reverse might have taken place in an Italian madrigal such as *O tu, cara scientia mia, musica*, where a small harp could play a simplified version of both voices simultaneously. He also recommends trying the Machaut Mass with voices performing a simplified version of the music, while instruments play the original. (See Ex. 23, p.146).

Some of the most exhaustive accounts of medieval instruments and their role in both secular and church music may be found in the published writings of Edmund A. Bowles. His *Musical Life and Performance Practices in the Fifteenth Century* (Leipzig, 1968) provides a wealth of pictorial background to a fruitful discussion of literary sources. Also of interest are the theories advanced in his 'Haut and Bas: the Grouping of Musical Instruments in the Middle Ages', *Musica Disciplina* VIII (1954), 115-140; 'The Role of Musical Instruments in Medieval Sacred Drama', *The Musical Quarterly* XLV (1959), 67-84; 'Musical Instruments in Civil Processions during the Middle Ages', *Acta Musicologica* XXXII (1961), 147-161. The terms 'haut' and 'bas', meaning loud and soft, usefully point to the different kinds of scoring used for certain events – trumpets and drums before a banquet, softer-toned woodwinds as a post-prandial diversion. But both

Ex. 23

kinds of instruments were used in processions and in mystery plays, also in dances and some liturgical services. A special study of the 'haut' category, to which is appended an invaluable list of manuscript illuminations and the instruments depicted, may be found in Dr Bowles' article 'Iconography as a Tool for Examining the Loud Consort in the Fifteenth Century', *Journal of the American Musical Instruments Society* III (1977), 100-121. The special demands of processional music are also discussed authoritatively in Heinrich Besseler's 'Umgangsmusik und Darbietungsmusik', *Archiv für Musikwissenschaft* XVI

(1959), 21-43, followed by a supplement of illustrations taken from tapestries, miniatures and paintings.

Many scholars agree that instrumental participation in church music was generally limited to the organ, or to a sustaining pair of wind or strings. In support of documentary and pictorial evidence is the survival of some twenty compositions ranging from Philippe de Vitry to Guillaume Dufay, all of which contain a 'solus tenor' – a continuous supporting melodic line acting as a conflation of tenor and contratenor. Whereas the tenor and contratenor could be played by sackbuts, for instance, because the playing and resting periods are staggered, the solus tenor is clearly intended for an instrument untrammeled by restrictions of breathing, such as a tenor viol, hurdy-gurdy or organ. One of the earliest known examples is the motet based on *Jacet granum*, in honour of Thomas Becket (from *Music in Honour of St Thomas of Canterbury* (Novello, London, 1970):

Ex. 24

147

Thus there are two basic possibilities for performance: two voices and a pair of sackbuts, or two voices and organ. This is also the case with other motets of this type, which are listed at the end of an article by Shelley Davis, 'The Solus Tenor in the 14th and 15th Centuries', *Acta Musicologica* XXXIX (1967), 44-64, with an Addendum in the same journal, XL (1968), 176-178. It should be noted however that the description of Pycard's *Gloria* (Old Hall MS, f. 23v-24) is not quite accurate since the tenor and contratenor are not in canon, and they do perform simultaneously. This motet ranks as a special case, since the solus tenor is not a conflate of two melodically different parts, but rather a continuous version of a single line which tenor and contratenor present in a kind of slow hocket, or broken version. Note also that the apparently conflicting nature of the key-signatures makes perfectly good musical sense when due attention is paid to the resolution of musica ficta problems. These are discussed in the first section of chapter 11 (pp.173–183).

Ex. 25

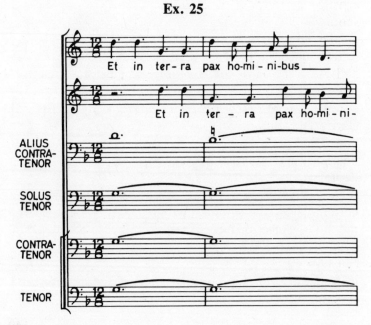

In the typical chanson texture of the early Renaissance a solo voice supported by two melodic lines tends to predominate. Whatever may or may not be gleaned from the artistic *bizarreries* of the age, it is essential that the poem should be clearly heard, and to that end excessive doubling of the voice-part should be avoided. One single soft instrument is quite sufficient, be it blown, bowed, or plucked. As to the tenor and the contratenor, which are essentially harmonic in function and purpose, each deserves to enjoy the continuous and steady kind of tone that will clarify the contours and provide a firm support to the upper line. The basic possibilities therefore consist of two viols, one on each part; or two wind instruments similarly deployed. A 'broken consort' is also often effective, slightly stressing the individual nature of the parts. It is better to avoid the temptation to use a lute alone for one of the lines, since that part will tend to recede both in dynamics and sustaining power. On the other hand, a lute can add delicate touches of colour when used as a doubling instrument, either for one or for two lines, according to the texture.

The performance of church music poses special problems, because the presence or absence of instruments depended on local customs, budgets, and circumstances. In a masterly study of 'Performance Practices at the Cathedral of Cambrai, 1475-1550', *The Musical Quarterly* LXIV (1978), 295-328, Craig Wright maintains that polyphony was sung without the assistance of instruments, and that even an organ was lacking. But he also points out that for special occasions – at a court chapel, a royal wedding, a ceremonial meeting as at the Field of Cloth of Gold, a Mass attended by royalty – minstrels and players on the cornett, sackbut, fife, trumpet and clarion could sometimes be heard. And the flutes, trumpets and organ were heard at the wedding of Maximilian I and Bianca Maria Sforza in the cathedral of Milan in 1493, if we can believe Beatrice d'Este Sforza's letter to her sister Isabella Gonzaga. The whole point about these varying traditions was that one and the same composition frequently had to serve at different times and places, and was modified accordingly in certain details. In exactly the same way a travelling opera or ballet company today will usually carry an orchestra of reduced size, and the amply orchestrated original scores have to be re-arranged to fit what is available.

A clear example of this custom may be deduced not from documentation or iconography but from the music itself, in the *Credo* by Guillaume Legrant preserved in two north Italian sources: Oxford, Bodleian Library, Canonici misc. 213, and Bologna, Civico Museo Bibliografico Musicale, MS. Q 15. The versions contained in these two closely related sources are collated in Van den Borren's Polyphonia Sacra (xxviii-xxx) and the music is presented after the Oxford version (127-133), in which the singable tenor and the uncomfortably angular contratenor are provided with text. In the Bologna manuscript, these two parts are devoid of text (other than brief cues), and what is more they feature a greater number of ligatures. Now the Bologna manuscript was probably compiled in Piacenza, while Venice was the home of the collection that found its

way to Oxford, and between Piacenza and Venice performance practices evidently differed. While the tenor part
could be either vocal or instrumental, the contratenor
seems to suggest a sackbut rather than voices:

Ex. 26

According to Frank D'Accone – 'The Performance of
Sacred Music in Italy', in *Josquin des Prez* (London, 1976),
601-618 — there are no records of instrumental participation in church music of Josquin's time as far as purely
liturgical services are concerned. The organ is mentioned
in archival sources, but nothing else, though by the 1560s it
was customary to hire a trombone player for services in San
Petronio, Bologna, and in the cathedrals of Modena and
Padua. The same volume contains interesting but inconclu-
sive discussions about the use of a trombone to bring out a
cantus firmus part in a Mass or motet (623, 624, 639).

There is one practical disadvantage in employing
instruments (even the organ) in this manner, as I discov-

ered many years ago when recording the *Missa Caput* then ascribed to Dufay. When the cantus firmus (and trombone) drop out of the texture, as they do from time to time, the singers must be able to stay perfectly on pitch. Should they fail to do so, even by a fraction of a semitone, the next instrumental entry will cause severe problems. When the pitch is stable – or is made so by the permanent presence of doubling instruments on the other parts – anxiety disappears, but at the expense of a possibly over-rich vocal-instrumental texture that may not be too accurate a reflection of historical circumstances. It is therefore a question of aesthetics, practicality, and fidelity; and the director must make up his mind.

In the later Renaissance, there is ample evidence for doubling vocal lines with instruments, a technique that came to be called *a cappella*, at one time confused with the term 'unaccompanied', which is quite different. Choirmasters could and did make use of instruments to double or to replace voices, some sets of printed partbooks even bearing annotations to this effect. Occasions of state, invariably provided with special music, as Albert Dunning has shown in his pioneering study *Die Staatsmotette, 1480-1555* (Utrecht, 1970), helped to loosen purse-strings and so make it possible to engage numerous instrumentalists. A little-known article by Alessandro Luzio, 'Isabella d'Este e i Borgia', *Archivio Storico Lombardo* XLII (1915), 164, includes a letter dated 18 February 1509 from a correspondent at the court of Ferrara to Isabella, then in Mantua, about a set of intermezzi written for the play *Phormione*, featuring *sordine* (perhaps *sordone*, a forerunner of the bassoon), lutes and various other instruments used for illustrative purposes and for dancing. A later report concerning a banquet given to Prospero Colonna in 1513 mentions not only the succession of fastidious culinary triumphs, but also the music that was heard – lutes, 'violoni', cornetti and 'pivi'. But for a description of what must surely have ranked among the most elaborately musical repasts of all time, we must turn to Christoforo di

Messisbugo's cook-book, *Banchetti, compositioni di vivande et apparechio generale* (first edition, 1549), which offers a lively account of banquets given at Ferrara in January and May, 1529. These accounts are valuable in that they show the great variety of instruments in use and the particular assignments given to them. Detailed descriptions may be found in three basic articles: José Llorens, 'Estudio de los instrumentos musicales que aparecen descritos en la relacion de dos festines celebrados el año 1529 en la corte de Ferrara', *Anuario Musical* XXV (1970), pp. 3-26; Howard M. Brown, 'A Cook's Tour of Ferrara in 1529', *Rivista Italiana di Musicologia* X (1975), pp. 216-241, and Pierre Tagmann, 'Ferraras Festivitäten von 1529', *Schweizer Beiträge zur Musikwissenschaft*, 3 (1978), pp. 85-105.

Florence too could underwrite magnificent musical spectacles. In the festivities for the marriage of Cosimo I and Eleonora of Toledo in 1539, the prologue and intermezzi for a play called for elaborate musical participation – and for once the exact scoring was specified. Full details of this, with the music and the historical background, are given in *A Renaissance Entertainment*, by Andrew C. Minor and Bonner Mitchell (University of Missouri Press, 1968). A later and possibly more splendid event was the entertainment for the marriage of Ferdinando de' Medici and Christine of Lorraine in 1589, with music by Marenzio, Malvezzi, and others. Here again the music has survived complete, along with careful descriptions of the instrumentation, reprinted in *Musique des Intermèdes de la Pellegrina*, edited by D.P. Walker (Paris, 1963) and discussed in Howard M. Brown, *Sixteenth Century Instrumentation* (Rome, 1975). Those attempting to use the Walker edition should note that the two accounts of the instrumentation sometimes differ; and that while Rossi is a person, Nono (though a perfectly good Italian family name) is not. Nono simply refers to the Ninth of a set of 14 partbooks, and it is there that the description is found. This material is summarized between pages XXXVII— LVIII and given in full in vol. 2.

Further useful material on the orchestration of inter-mezzi may be found in an article by Robert L. Weaver: 'Sixteenth-Century Instrumentation', *The Musical Quarterly* XLVII (1961), 363-378, in which the last few pages offer a conspectus of the art from 1475 to 1599 in a quick-reference tabular form.

It is in many ways unfortunate that the basic 16th century textbook on the art of combining instruments into a viable ensemble continues to elude those who would benefit most from studying it. The book in question is *Il Desiderio* (first edition, Venice, 1594), named for one of the two discussants, Gratioso Desiderio, a nom-de-plume of the true author, Ercole Bottrigari, who was a wealthy and erudite Bolognese nobleman. The other party to this musical dialogue, Annibale Melone, excelled as a practising musician and was a great friend of Bottrigari, who insisted at first on publishing the book under Melone's name in the form of an anagram, Alemanno Benel[l]i. A coruscating cornucopia of information about instrumental practices of the time, especially those associated with the city and court of Ferrara (where Bottrigari lived for eleven years), *Il Desiderio* deals especially with the correct way in which instruments should be combined in concert.*

Instead of being thrown together as is frequently done in modern concerts and recordings, the instruments should – according to Bottrigari – be grouped according to their individual characteristics in tuning and temperament. Three principal categories exist: stable instruments, which (once tuned) cannot be altered, such as organs, harpsichords, spinets and double harps; stable but alterable, referring to fretted instruments such as the lute, viol, flutes, cornetts, all capable of sensitive modifications of pitch; and finally the completely alterable group – trombones, rebecs and the pear-shaped lira. Thoughtlessly combined, these instruments would produce 'a real *concerto*, or battle,

---

* For information on violins in Renaissance consorts see the chapter 'Early History' in Menuhin and Primrose, *Violin and Viola* (London 1976), pp. 193-220.

instead of a *concento*, a union and concord of diverse voices and sounds': yet there follows such a detailed discussion of pitch and temperament that it soon becomes clear that ways and means could be found to overcome at least some of the apparent obstacles. The entire book deserves close study, and very fortunately the difficult Italian has been translated with clarity and brilliance by Carol MacClintock in her edition of 1962 in the series *Musicological Studies and Documents*, No. 9, American Institute of Musicology (Rome).

The Baroque and After

If Bottrigari's attitude to instrumentation reflected late 16th century practice in Italy at such musically well-endowed courts as Ferrara, it was the lead given by the Sienese Agostino Agazzari in his treatise of 1607 – *Del sonare sopra 'l basso con tutti li stromenti e dell' uso loro nel conserto* – that helped to launch the new sound and the new look of the baroque orchestra. Agazzari's advice is translated into English in Oliver Strunk's *Source Readings in Music History* (London and New York, 1950), and its timely message is elaborated upon by Gloria Rose in her article 'Agazzari and the Improvising Orchestra', *Journal of the American Musicological Society* XVIII (1965), 382-393. Unlike Bottrigari, who classifies instruments according to temperament, Agazzari divides them according to their function: they are either foundation instruments, charged with filling in the harmonies suggested by the *basso seguente*, or else they are ornamental, enlivening the middle and upper parts with a certain amount of improvised embellishment. His descriptions of the possibilities and characteristics of each instrument are worthy of careful consideration, as are his warnings about the danger of over-doing frills and fripperies: a soloist must lead the ensemble, but if at some other time he is part of a group, then he and his colleagues must pay attention to each other, not shout each other down like so many hungry sparrows.

The year in which Agazzari's advice was published also saw the première of Monteverdi's *Orfeo* in Mantua, to be followed by the appearance of a full score destined to serve many composers seeking for ideas and techniques in a relatively new art. The accent was upon colour, variety, and blending of sound; even in distant London, a few weeks prior to *Orfeo*, Thomas Campion's masque in honour of Lord Hay and his bride made full use of a rich orchestral palette. One ensemble of ten musicians included a pair of violins (and perhaps other members of the family)' accompanied by a continuo section that would certainly have pleased Agazzari, for there was a harpsichord, a bass sackbut, two lutes and a bandora. A second ensemble also boasted a continuo section of three lutes and bass viol supporting upper strings, while a third mixed voices and cornets, six of each, 'in a place raised higher in respect of the piercing sound of these instruments'.

This early indication of concern for balance finds echoes in various later writings. Monteverdi's letter of 9 December 1616 to Alessandro Striggio, with its thinly-veiled disapproval of the maritime fable *Le Nozze di Tetide*, stresses the enormous problems of balance attendant upon a stage situation in which the continuo instruments would have to be placed far back, necessitating many extra instruments and therefore the danger of forcing the voices. Monteverdi's friend, Giovanni Battista Doni, followed the same general line in his *Trattato della musica scenica* (written about 1635):

> As for the custom of using so many different kinds of instruments to make a filling, as they say . . . it provides so little sound that it can hardly be heard by those nearest the stage . . . with the result that their sound, at the very most, reaches the ears of those who are in the middle of the hall. But if it is so loud that it can reach the far end, it will cover the voices too much (and they are usually heard but little), while those who are in the front seats will be unable to endure it.

One of the most important questions that the choir director had to face was this problem of balance, together with the special peculiarities of combining voices with instruments in church music. But he was by no means lacking in assistance and advice, above all in northern Italy where the cross-surge of *cori spezzati* had forced the formulation of new colouristic concepts. Girolamo Giacobbi, an eminent Bolognese composer, included a *Magnificat* in eighteen parts scored for five choirs in his *Salmi concertati* of 1609, and one of his favourite ideas was the cultivation of 'distant singing' whereby groups of musicians were placed at some distance from the main chorus or choruses.

Three years later, in 1612, this method received further approval in publications of Lodovico Grossi da Viadana (*Salmi à 4 Chori per cantare e concertare*), Ignatio Donati (*Sacri concentus*), and Giovanni Battista Fergusio (*Motetti e Dialoghi*). At the time, Viadana was in charge of the music at the cathedral of Fano, only a few miles along the Adriatic coast from Pesaro, where Donati served as choir director. Apparently they both experimented with far-flung combinations of voices and instruments, as did the lawyer and amateur composer Fergusio, who lived in Savigliano south of Turin. It was clearly a widespread movement enjoying much support from musicians of all types.

Viadana's advice appears in the form of a full page of detailed instructions entitled 'Modo di concertare i detti salmi a quattro chori'. They may be summarized as follows:

> *Choir 1.* To be placed near the main organ, this 'coro favorito' is no choir at all, but rather a group of five first-rate soloists, having no accompaniment other than the organ and possibly a chitarrone. The organist is expressly warned not to indulge in ornamentation.
> *Choir 2.* This forms the basis of the harmony and should consist of not less than 16 singers. If the number ranges between 20 and 30 (including instrumentalists), so much the better.

Choir 3. High range; with cornetto or violin doubling the top line, 1-3 castrati on the second line, some mezzi-soprani with violins and krummhorns on the third, and tenor voices, trombones, cellos, and portative organ on the lowest.

Choir 4. Low range; with low alto (several voices), violins at the upper octave, and krummhorns on the top line, several tenors and trombones on the second line, baritones, trombone and cello on the third, and many low basses, trombones, double-bass and bassoons on the lowest.

This cannot have been far removed from the Venetian practice of Andrea and Giovanni Gabrieli, neither of whom left specific instructions as to how their music might be scored, although a polychoral work such as Giovanni's *Omnes gentes plaudite manibus*, or his uncle's *Gloria* for four choirs, would sound quite splendid if arranged along the lines suggested by Viadana. The practice seems to have been well known in Cremona at least as early as 1614, when on 16 November (Translation of St Omobono) a motet in his honour was performed at the cathedral. No less than four choirs and a group of strings and trombones, under the direction of the composer Nicolo Corradino, bedazzled the congregation with the ritornels and verses of *Jocundare tu Cremona / Homoboni pro corona*, if we may believe the account of the historian Giuseppe Bresciani who was present at the ceremony.

Music on stage was for obvious reasons less predictable than that intended for public worship. Each opera, intermezzo or masque required music to fit its list of characters and scenes. So it was that in the very year of the Cremonese motet referred to above, *The Masque of Flowers* (with music by John Wilson) featured a choral dialogue between the followers of Silenus (Bacchus) and Kawasha, a devotee of tobacco:

Before Silenus marched four singers, and behind him five fiddlers; before and behind Kawasha as many of each kind. The singers on Silenus' part were a miller, a wine cooper, a vintner's boy, a brewer. His music, a tabor and a pipe, a bass violin, a treble violin, a sackbut, a mandora. Kawasha's singers, a skipper, a fencer, a pedlar, a barber. His music, a bobtail, a blind harper and his boy, a bass violin, a tenor cornett, a sackbut.

On 21 November of the following year, 1615, Monteverdi wrote one of his best-known letters to Annibale Iberti, a court official at Mantua, where the ballet *Tirsi e Clori* was shortly to be performed. The music was later published in the Seventh Book of Madrigals (1619) but without any hint as regards scoring, a lacuna which is fortunately filled by this letter:

> If by good fortune the enclosed [ballet] should be to His Highness's liking, I would think it proper to perform it in a half-moon, at whose corners should be placed an archlute and a harpsichord, one each side, one playing the bass for Chloris and the other for Thyrsis, each of them holding a lute, and playing and singing themselves to their own instruments and to the afore-mentioned. If there could be a harp instead of a lute for Chloris, that would be even better. Then, having reached the ballet movement after they have sung a dialogue, there could be added to the ballet six more voices in order to make eight voices in all, eight viole da braccio, a contrabass, a spineta arpata, and if there were also two lutes, that would be fine. And directed with a beat suitable to the character of the melodies, avoiding over-excitement among the singers and players, and with the understanding of the ballet-master, I hope that – sung in this way – it will not displease His Highness.

The name of Michael Praetorius is frequently invoked as an authority in matters of orchestration, and while it is true that his *Syntagma Musicum* (Part III, 1619) offers much useful information, a considerable part of it is taken (as he

159

himself admits) from Giacobbi, Viadana, and from the Somascan Father, Giuseppe Gallo of Milan, whose encomiastic preface to the *Sacri operis musici* of 1598 seems to have inspired the German master to list all the instruments capable of doubling voices from high soprano down to low bass. A too literal adherence to Praetorius has sometimes resulted in performances of Italian church music that suffer from a thick and heavy texture, making Soriano sound like Schumann and Monteverdi like Mahler, but when used with discretion his maxims often prove to be of value.

Another frequent error is the lamentable tendency to over-score revivals of Venetian operas, such as the later works of Monteverdi and those of Cavalli and Cesti. In the case of Cesti's *Pomo d'Oro*, which ranks as an occasional piece written for an imperial wedding in Vienna, the opulent scoring reflects the tone of the event, but the other works are generally scored for modest orchestral resources. A well-rounded introduction to theatrical music of the early baroque is Janet Beat's 'Monteverdi and the Opera Orchestra of his Time', in *The Monteverdi Companion*, edited by Denis Arnold and Nigel Fortune (London 1968), while more general aspects are discussed in *Venetian Instrumental Music from Gabrieli to Vivaldi*, by Eleanor Selfridge-Field (Oxford, 1975).

Once established, the orchestra developed its own rules and traditions which, though appreciably modified with the passing of time and the gradual perfection of instrument-making and performing technique, are very little changed in essence even in our own time. The main groups of strings, woodwind, brass and percussion still remain the foundations of colour and timbre that they always were, and no significant problems arise because the survival of autograph scores and first editions, giving complete details of scoring, is a matter of accepted musicological fact. If conductors alter the instrumentation of Bach, Mozart, Beethoven, Schumann, Mussorgsky – indeed of any creative individual whose wisdom might be called in question –

they do so not in the spirit of the old *maestro di cappella*, but rather because the resources of the modern orchestra tempt them to interfere and 'improve'. Frederick Stock and others improved on Schumann's orchestration, Weingartner on Beethoven's, though late in his life he relented. Levi, Nikisch, Schalk and Loewe all had a hand in revising Bruckner's symphonies, not only as regards their scoring but even in their formal structure. In more recent times, Stokowski loved to tamper with balance and colour, especially in recording sessions where, in any event, electronic artificialities can be introduced at the flip of a switch. At a rehearsal of Sibelius's Symphony No. 2, I witnessed with some amusement a series of experiments conducted by Sir Thomas Beecham, who was plainly dissatisfied with the sound of the five-note bass motive at letter N of the slow movement. Finally the principal cellist was invited to play the phrase an octave higher, upon which Sir Thomas announced with a beatific smile that he wished he had time to re-orchestrate all the works of the great composers.

It is only fair to state that, purism apart, certain special cases do call for drastic remedies, and one of these perhaps is the music of Frederick Delius, which Beecham brought to the world in a way that was unrivalled and unsurpassed for its magical insight, its legendary sensitivity. At a very early stage in their relationship he sized up the situation, and after first approaching it cautiously, he soon launched what amounted to a full-scale campaign, as he tells us in *A Mingled Chime*:

> . . . it was during these periods of relaxation that I would lead him to talk about his music and the correct interpretation of it. So far he had never been present at either rehearsals or performances where I had given any of his works, and I was not yet sure that I had been doing the right thing by them. The scores, especially the printed ones, were vilely edited and annotated, and if played in exact accordance with their directions of tempo, phrasing, and dynamics

could not help being comparatively ineffective and unconvincing.

The mental and mechanical aspects of the campaign have been succinctly described by two men who knew Beecham's methods down to the last detail. Their accounts are given in Humphrey Procter-Gregg's *Sir Thomas Beecham: Conductor and Impresario* (privately printed, 1974), and the first is by Eric Fenby:

> The basic details had been pondered beforehand. He would mark every bar of the score in blue pencil, exaggerating Delius's own nuances of expression, to make the fullest impact in performance. Copyists would then transfer these markings to each of the orchestral parts of the works. . . . His chief concern with Delius was in tending the melodic strands that pass from voice to voice and give the piece its form, and, no less important, the balancing of timbres carrying the supporting harmonies.

If there is many a slip 'twixt the cup and the lip, there was (in Beecham's case) many a change between rehearsal and performance, proving beyond a shadow of doubt that he was sensitive to the often subtle differences between one hall and another, or this and that orchestra. The second writer is Douglas Steele, who began his association with Beecham in 1939:

> . . . there were hundreds of small details relating to dynamics, phrasing and so on, which went into the parts in different coloured pencils. When I had marked them for a Sunday afternoon performance of Delius's *Paris*, which took place in the Queen's Hall, the rehearsal revealed a series of shadings leading to the wonderful oboe melody, which did not yet absolutely satisfy Sir Thomas. We had spent hours transmitting into the parts, already heavily marked, indications for a slightly different tempo, and a series of complicated and most carefully graded diminuendos.

> Before the concert, we were summoned to Sir
> Thomas, and given a mass of entirely new instruc-
> tions. . . . And so we would get our coats off, and start
> again.

Nobody can prove that this kind of thing did not also take
place in earlier times, for works tend to survive in presentation copies rather than in the form of actual material used
in performances. If we can believe Monteverdi when he
asserts, in his letter dated 9 January 1620, that *Arianna*
needed five months of strenuous rehearsals after the pre-
liminary work of committing it to memory, we must also
assume that a fair proportion of this period was given up to
the marking of music, the writing in of expression, dynamics, ornamentation; and that some of these had to be
modified or improved upon when the time came for stage
rehearsals.

The search for true authenticity in scoring and sound can
sometimes turn out to be long, arduous, and relatively
unfruitful, simply because the magic recipe, once found,
can melt away in the blinding light of some equally valid
'discovery' made by someone else working on entirely
independent lines. There is no single answer to the problem. Nevertheless, intelligent guesses are better than
nothing, though they ought to be extended far beyond the
'early music' field up to the classical and romantic repertoire, so that audiences can hear orchestral music by
Haydn, Mozart, Beethoven, Brahms and others with the
kind of wind and brass instruments current in those times.
Back to C clarinets, alto trombones, and ophicleides –
indeed this has been done recently in conductorless performances of the Eroica Symphony and the repertoire of
the late 18th century, and there is every indication that the
cult of *Aufführungspraxis* will bring a few more surprises in
the years to come. *Plus ça change, plus c'est la même chose*.

Ten
Vocal Tone-Colour

> ... the English doe carroll; the French
> sing; the Spaniards weepe; the Italians,
> which dwell about the Coasts of *Ianua*
> caper with their Voyces; the other barke:
> but the Germanes (which I am ashamed to
> utter) doe howle like Wolves.
>
> John Dowland: *Andreas Ornithoparcus*
> *His Micrologus*

Tinctoris and Aron, among others, found it expedient to
comment upon national vocal characteristics in language
almost as bizarre as that of Ornithoparcus, but their pro-
nouncements belong more to the realm of the epigram-
matic than the epic – especially the remark about the
capering Genoese, and the unfair judgement on the Ger-
mans. Of course there are times when a trick of pronuncia-
tion or voice-production will reveal the nationality of a
singer, yet who has not occasionally been deceived by the
superb artistry of a musician who knows how to enter into
the spirit of declamation and timbre that may be foreign to
him, or to her?

For artistry of the highest order is at the root of all
successful vocal interpretation, and it has been so from
time immemorial. The fortunate owners of voices that
combine the virtues of beauty, power, accuracy and clarity
have been consistently praised down the centuries, and in
terms not far removed from those employed by Isidore,
Archbishop of Seville, in his *Etymologiarium* (*c*. 630):

> The perfect voice is high, sweet and loud; high, to be
> adequate to the sublime; loud, to fill the ear; sweet, to
> soothe the minds of the hearers. If any one of these
> qualities is absent, the voice is not perfect.

Similar sentiments inform a poem attributed to Eugenio III, Bishop of Toledo, in the 10th-11th century Antiphoner of Léon as cited by Robert Stevenson in his *Spanish Music in the Age of Columbus* (The Hague, 1960), 14:

> Remove from the choir those with raucous voices,
> Those who refuse to apply what they have been taught,
> Those who burst their lungs and strain their throats,
> Those whose breath miserably gives out,
> Those who make an ugly noise like the braying of donkeys,
> Those whose wretched voices sound like the howling of wolves.
> Leave off such sounds and banish such voices . . .

The actual method of voice-production seems to have been of less consequence than its result in terms of tonal aesthetics, if we can believe Chaucer, whose Prioress – madame Englentyne – apparently favoured a nasal approach: 'Ful wel she sang the servisès divine / Entunèd in her nose ful swetely'. Perhaps she had been a novice in France.

A Practical Approach

It is a strange and sometimes depressing experience to watch a faulty theory gather unto itself large numbers of ill-informed practitioners, who find it much easier to accept dubious data than to question it. Some years ago an ideal for tone-production in early music was set up on the following slender basis: since the faces of singers in a certain painting seemed to have strained expressions and tight muscles, the tone-quality must have been reedy and nasal. Therefore most if not all the music of the Renaissance should be sung in this way, whether (*pace* Ornithoparcus) its executants were Italian, English, French, Spanish or German. (See Plate 8, p. 166).

Sad to say, this false theory generated enough in the way of blind support to colour recordings and performances for many years, and even now there are vestiges of its noxious tracks in certain quarters where better sense should prevail. Instead of hearing voices of perfect refinement and

Plate 8

Part of the van Eyck altar-piece at Ghent. Do the 'strained expressions' of the angels prove that their singing is harsh and without vibrato?

exquisite beauty, we were offered sounds reminiscent of a castrated ship-siren. Instead of hearing what the good archbishop Isidore would have described as 'an attractive voice, soft and flexible' (*vox vinnula*, from *vinnus* meaning a softly-curling lock of hair), we were obliged to listen – for as long as we could bear it – to a forced, hard, artificial type of sound which ill accords with early ear-witness reports of solo and ensemble singing as it was practised in the best musical circles, at home, at court, and in church.

This historical evidence amply demonstrates that the most admired singing, at whatever point in the flowering of western music, was that which incorporated strength, sweetness, flexibility, and other attributes of a positive nature. An Italian who listened to singers of the English Chapel Royal at Mass in the early 16th century found their voices 'more divine than human'. It is unlikely that they were forcing the tone, for many English writers of the time define vocal excellence in terms of smoothness and amiability. Richard Mulcaster (1581) tells us that 'music stands not so much upon straining or fullness of the voice, but is delicate and fine in concent' [i.e. *concentus*, or harmony]. And William Barley (1596), calls music 'a science which teacheth how to sing skilfully: that is, to deliver a song sweetly, tunably, and cunningly'. John Dowland's translation of Ornithoparcus assures us that 'God is not pleased with loud cries, but with lovely sounds'; and one such sound was so memorable as to find its way into the correspondence of the Duke of Württemberg, who heard Mattins at St George's Chapel, Windsor, one Sunday in 1592 and recalled that 'a young choirboy there sang so sweetly, and with such embellishment, that it was wonderful to listen to'.

In Germany, Heinrich Finck among many others recommended that the singer should make sure to employ

> a quality of voice as sweet, pleasing, smooth and polished as can be produced. The higher a voice rises, the quieter and more gentle should be the tone; the lower it goes, the richer should be the sound . . . with

the result that the counterpoint and harmony make their way evenly into the ear so that each voice sounds just as clear, gentle and smooth as any other, and the listeners enjoy the performance to the full and experience the appropriate emotion'.

Finck refers to polyphonic singing in that passage, and recommends a controlled dynamic level as being most suitable for that kind of performance. In solo singing, however, greater liberties could be taken, as is known from the numerous descriptions of Italian virtuosi in the second half of the 16th century. Vincenzo Giustiniani, writing about singers who were active about 1575, singles out three basses each with a range of over three octaves, and a variety of passage-work that was 'new and pleasing to all ears'. He then mentions the ladies of Mantua and Ferrara, who cultivated a subtle and expressive type of singing, for they 'moderated or increased their voices, loud or soft, heavy or light, according to the demands of the composition'. After a summer concert in Ferrara in 1571, a member of the audience described an ensemble of sixty voices and instruments, among whom Luzzaschi played the harpsichord and

Signora Lucrezia and Signora Isabella Bendidio sang, each alone and then the two together, so exquisitely and so smoothly that I do not believe that it would be possible to hear better.

A similar concert at Ferrara caused Alessandro Striggio the elder to compare the ladies to 'angels from paradise'. Apparently there were no harsh or unpleasing sounds there, nor in Rome where Ippolita Marrotta sang, nor in Florence where Francesca and Settimia Caccini vied with Virginia Archilei, nor in Mantua whither Duke Vincenzo had tempted the greatest of them all — Adriana Basile. Ademollo's ever-fascinating story of her life and art cites panegyrics in prose and poetry whose pardonable hyperbole contains not one shred of evidence that she ever sang other than with a pure, sweet and beautiful voice. And the same was true of the men, notably Monteverdi's pupil Campagnolo and the great Francesco Rasi, who (according to Severo Bonini) possessed a firm, suave voice, always beautiful and full of emotion and spirit.

What was thought to be impressive in Tuscany and Lombardy was also prized in Venice, especially when the voice was that of a high counter-tenor, so convincingly described by Thomas Coryate in his *Crudities* (1611), where he recalls music at Vespers on the Feast of S. Rocco:

> Of the singers there were three or four so excellent that I think few or none in Christendom do excel them, especially one, who had such a peerless and (as I may in a manner say) such a supernatural voice for sweetness, that I think there was never a better singer in all the world, insomuch that he did not only give the most pleasant contentment that could be imagined, to all the hearers, but also did (as it were) astonish and amaze them. I always thought he was an Eunuch, which if he had been, it had taken away some part of my admiration, because they do most commonly sing passing well; but he was not, therefore it was much the more admirable. Again, it was the more worthy of admiration, because he was a middle-aged man, as about 40 years old. For nature doth more commonly bestow such a singularity of voice upon boys and striplings, than upon men of such years. Besides, it was far the more excellent, because it was nothing forced, strained, or affected, but came from him with the greatest facility that ever I heard. Truly I think that, had a Nightingale been in the same room, and contended with him for the superiority, something perhaps he might excel him, because God hath granted that little bird such a privilege for the sweetness of his voice, as to none other; but I think he could not much.

Ercole Bottrigari, in *Il Desiderio*, gives us a glimpse of amateur singing groups in Bologna, and it seems that their ideals were not too far from those of our modern consorts or chamber choirs. Their methods too were somewhat like ours, for they believed in careful rehearsal, a choice of good music, criticism of each other, and (if need be) asking for professional assistance:

> Each member, having attended to his own affairs all day, gathered with the others in the evening; and after rehearsing certain of their songs they went forth together, and for several hours – sometimes before supper, sometimes after, and even up till the break of day – went wandering through the city greeting with their delightful songs now one, now another, now still another friend, all of whom were most consoled by it. And their desire to perfect this kind of harmony with perfect union was such that besides seeking many times the useful advice of the director of music at the cathedral, they never ceased to admonish each other most kindly about their own defects; and finally, standing close together and (wrapped in their mantles) almost hidden in darkness, they demonstrated that – as they were united as closely as possible with their bodies, of which they would indeed have wished to make one body only – likewise they delighted in making as far as they could a true union of their respective voices, from which came forth an almost celestial harmony.

Padre Martini enlarges upon these observations by pointing out that madrigals should be sung softly, and that the perfect intonation so necessary for bringing out bold dissonances is easier to achieve in a small group than in a larger one such as a church choir.

Vibrato

Those who advocate hard and strident vocal colour further sully their misconceptions by inveighing against vibrato, which is a relatively harmless tonal adjunct as long as it is kept in reasonable control. The swing of fashion has affected it from the earliest times, and its impact on vocal and instrumental music can be measured by listening to recordings made at various times during the present century. At first, violinists used little vibrato or none at all, but in course of time the vibrato dominated tone-production and (depending on its speed and width) sometimes came close to being an all-pervading nuisance. Recent years have witnessed a more balanced outlook, in which a controlled vibrato – along with a subtle ability to turn if off in order to point up some crucial note or phrase – plays a by no means unimportant part. Singers have also begun to display more sensitivity, abandoning the uninterrupted wobble for a much more expressive and intelligently deployed vibrato that does not noticeably affect accuracy of intonation.

This historical evidence proves that vibrato was cultivated and appreciated, especially as an intensifier of expressive effects, of which the Antiphoner of Léon offers a splendid example. In the solemn liturgy for Good Friday, at the beginning of the *Improperia* (Reproaches), the bishop is directed to sing 'Popule meus, quid feci tibi' with a tremolo in his voice (*voce tremula*), a term which appears later in secular music. It is true that Franchino Gafforio, in his *Practica Musicae* (Milan, 1496), advises members of church choirs to avoid using a wide and ringing vibrato, which destroys pitch and therefore spoils perfect concord with other voices, but by implication he allows a small and non-ringing vibrato – that is, a controlled one. Teofilo Folengo, the Mantuan poet who chose to publish his *Macaroneae* of 1516 under the assumed name of 'Merlinus Cocaius', speaks of Flemish singers who

> having drunk good wine, begin to sing with vibrant voices, which their throats may very easily send forth since they are all strong and robust in the breast.

Among documentary evidence in favour of the vibrato is an account by Frederic Gershow, a member of the Duke of

Stettin's entourage, of a visit to the Blackfriars Theatre in 1602, where he heard music before the beginning of the play. In addition to an instrumental piece there was a song for treble voice and bass viol, prompting Gershow's praise of the boy for singing with vibrato (*cum voce tremula*). In the Third Book of his *Syntagma Musicum* (1619), Praetorius mentions as the first of three pre-requisites for a fine natural voice 'a beautiful, attractive, trembling and wavering sound', though he hastens to add that this should be used in moderation.

In modern revivals of early music, vibrato must not be ruled out altogether. It should be used carefully in solo music, and always with expressive qualities in view – for example when strongly contrasting words such as 'heat' and 'cold' occur in the text, as they often do in lyric poetry of the Renaissance. In ensemble music for solo voices such as a five-voice madrigal, a natural vibrato is not out of place provided the individual singers exercise control and taste. Again, the sentiment of the text can be a useful guide, as can the musical context and texture. Bold changes of harmony in the works of Rore, de Wert, Gesualdo, Nenna, Monteverdi, and Sigismondo d'India fail to make their full impact unless vibrato is turned off momentarily, but when the safety of a more diatonic road is reached, a warmth of tone created by just the right trace of vibrato will serve to add colour and contrast. Cadences should also be treated with respect, especially those in which all voices converge on a single note or an open fifth, for it is at these points that a non-vibrato effect provides the best possible vehicle for the composer's message.

Eleven
Musical Pitfalls

> Many voices of men and women joined in
> deeper bass with the shrill tenor of the
> choral urchins.
>
> Edward Bulwer-Lytton: *The Last of the
> Barons*

The existence of an alarming number of misprints in ostensibly reliable scores of classical, romantic, and modern works will be readily apparent to all who know Norman Del Mar's articles 'Confusion and Error', *The Score* no. 21 (October 1957), and no. 22 (February 1958), the revisions of Haydn by H.C. Robbins Landon, and of Verdi and Puccini by Denis Vaughan. Early music too has its share of misprints and pitfalls, for the chain of events spanning conception and performance is that much greater than in modern times. Composers usually worked from an erasable *cartella*, each section of the score being immediately transferred to parts, which explains why – in manuscript and printed editions from the 16th to the 18th century – partbooks are far and away more numerous than scores.

Musica Ficta

At rehearsals, it was not uncommon for musicians and directors to make changes, especially in *musica ficta* (the addition of flats and sharps to modify the line and harmony); and if printed material thus altered were later re-copied by hand, which sometimes happened, further errors might easily occur. Re-transcribed and edited in our own times, these early sources once again become the possible victims of errors, mis-transcriptions and proof-reading mistakes, so that the sum total of all this transference of material from inspiration to interpretation can be very considerable.

There are two escape routes for the musician anxious to avoid trouble of this kind. One leads to primary sources in the great research libraries, and is liable to consume both time and money on an unimaginable scale, while the other calls for the exercise of a little musical common-sense, which apart from being less expensive can sometime yield superior results. The art is in developing an inner ear, in tune with that of the composer, and an X-ray eye capable of penetrating to the source of the error. Example 27 shows five compositions ranging from the 13th to the 16th century, as they are printed in modern scholarly editions:

Ex. 27(a, b, c, d, e)

Excerpt (a), from a Worcester manuscript, is in dire need of *ficta* flats, and Machaut (b) requires further experimentation with regard to the entry-point of the second and third voices. The opening duo of a Ciconia motet (c) sounds better when the two voices begin together (and when the fifth note of the lower voice is read as C, not D, for even sacrosanct manuscripts contain egregious errors). Neusidler's *Judentanz* (d) becomes intelligible when the upper string of the lute is tuned a semitone higher according to instructions, while Cabezon's *Pavana* (e) loses its awkward five-bar phrase when bars 2-4 are treated as a hemiola by removing the dots. It would be possible to cite dozens of similar examples whose oddities derive from some misinterpretation or other, but the above will serve to advocate watchfulness at all times, and a healthy suspicion of all editors.

The topic of pitch is of course extremely tiresome because no matter how much is written about it masterpieces of past eras continue to be performed either too high or too low, and this applies just as well to medieval polyphony as to Bach's *St John Passion*. The most recent summary of the situation is Arthur Mendel's 'Pitch in Western Music since 1500 — a Re-examination', *Acta Musicologica* L (1978), 1-92. Discussing the theories of David Wulstan, as expressed in 'The Problem of Pitch in Sixteenth-century English Vocal Music', *Proceedings of the Royal Musical Association* 93 (1966-67), 97-112, Mendel admits that the 'generous application of common sense to bothersome complexities – clearly based on much knowledge and thought as it is – must appeal to those who prefer not to entertain doubts and "get on with it" '. In all fairness to some of the old theorists, their rebarbative wordiness can sometimes enshrine a perfect little gem of sensible advice, as when Ganassi (*Regola Rubertina*, chapter XI) recommends setting vocal pitch by working from the lowest note in the bass part and making this fit the lowest note that your bass singer (or singers) can comfortably produce.

In his *Dialogo della musica antica e della moderna*, Vincenzo Galilei severely criticizes those who transpose music to outlandish pitches that are

> unsingable, altogether out of the ordinary, and full of artifice; and this only in order to vaunt themselves and their achievements as miracles before those more ignorant than themselves.

The most practical way to approach the problem in unaccompanied vocal music is to go through each part and discover its extreme ranges, high and low; then to apply a transposition that permits each voice to sing within its normal and effective range. That range will vary slightly between one ensemble and another, and between one singer and another, and for this reason no set mathematical formula can possibly cover all eventualities. A useful upper limit for sopranos and tenors is G, which is not to say that notes above that limit cannot be tolerated; though they might begin to sound slightly operatic. It must also be borne in mind that even when the work has been adjusted for the best possible tessitura, some voice-part – written perhaps for exceptional singers, as in the case of certain works by de Wert, Monteverdi, and Schütz, to name but three composers – may require special treatment, as when an otherwise normal soprano part runs down to the alto range, or when a fairly well-behaved alto decides to sing tenor. In some cases parts can be exchanged for a few bars if the medium is a vocal consort; or in a chamber choir some kind of subtle dove-tailing and tone-matching will take care of the matter. An arrangement of this kind is shown in Ex. 28, from Monteverdi's *Quell' augellin che canta*, in which the original alto line descends all the way down to tenor C – quite out of the question for contraltos and counter-tenors, unless they have extraordinary voices.

Ex. 28

From Monteverdi: *Ten Madrigals for Mixed Voices* (edited by Denis Stevens). By permission of Oxford University Press.

The use of *musica ficta* was a thorny question when it first came up in the Middle Ages, and if the thorns have now been exchanged for hypodermic needles dispensing editorial pain-killer the basic problem still remains, for it is partly a matter of individual taste, partly of sensitivity to style. What sits well with Machaut may be uncomfortable with Josquin, and Josquin is not without his problems as may be seen in the following sequence from his *Déploration d'Ockeghem*, after the Susato edition of 1545:

Ex. 29

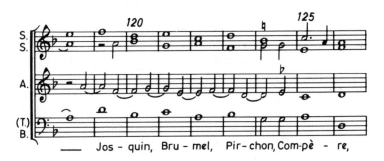

Jos - quin, Bru - mel, Pir - chon, Com-pè - re,

Some profess themselves alarmed by the momentary 'diminished fifth chord' in the second half of bar 124, though whether the composer thought in terms of chords is dubious to say the least. In the sequential context it can hardly be described as offensive. But subtle variations are possible, since natural notes can be flattened, and flats can be raised a semitone. The version in the Medici Codex, in fact, flattens the 'offending' E in the alto part (shown as a *ficta* flat in Ex. 29), but this causes a false relation with the next chord: E ♭ major followed immediately by A minor! The pundits shake their heads in despair. Yet there is an alternate solution – a simple, logical, and characteristic one, which is to leave the alto E ♮ alone and give a *ficta* natural to the soprano B ♭, resulting in a more singable melodic line which avoids the tritone E-B ♭ (121-124). The cross-relation between bass in 123 and soprano in 124 is both natural and effective.

It must be borne in mind at all times that *ficta* is subject to fashion, new styles appearing every decade or so. Greater distance brings greater divergence, as may be seen in two versions of a cadence in Dufay's chanson *Bien doy servir*. The first is from *Denkmäler der Tonkunst in Österreich*, XI[1] (Vienna, 1904), 78; the second is found in Besseler's complete edition, VI (Rome, 1964), 37.

The unsatisfactory nature of Ex. 30a is caused by a failure to recognize and understand the implications of the 'conflicting' key-signatures (as they are sometimes, though misleadingly called) for there is an inherent logic in the use of a B ♭ in the lower parts, and no flat in the upper part. Early Renaissance harmony came about as a result of horizontal – or contrapuntal – thought whose prop and mainstay was the concept of mode; and since the average tessitura of an alto line was approximately a fifth above a tenor line, composers found no conflict in allowing the key-signatures to reflect this difference of a fifth. Nevertheless, as in the case of Josquin cited above, flattening notes is only one of two alternatives. Adding a flat to the alto B softened the descent of Dufay's line to the F; but the editor should have reacted to the typical 15th-century cadence (the octave-leap cadence of the middle voice, coupled with the implied leading-note of the top voice) by adding sharps and naturals as Besseler has done, thus easing the harmony into a fitting V-I close, as in Ex. 30b:

Ex. 30 (a, b)

If theorists made life difficult, singers were often worse offenders. That they enjoyed adding *ficta* to their own lines, usually without regard to what their neighbours might or might not be singing, is perfectly clear from an eye- and ear-witness account of a heated discussion that took place during a rehearsal of Escribano's *Lamentations* at some time between 1538 and 1544. The documents consist of three manuscripts in the Biblioteca Vallicelliana, Rome, presenting versions of an essay on music by Ghiselin Danckerts, a papal singer. A useful article on these sources is Lewis Lockwood's 'A Dispute on Accidentals in Sixteenth-Century Rome', *Analecta Musicologica* II (1965), 24-40. The musicians involved were members of the choir of S. Lorenzo in Damaso, a church built into the fabric of the former papal chancellery, and the dispute apparently arose because certain singers were adding accidentals to their parts, overlooking the fact that polyphony is a complex web of sounds worthy of intelligent and thoughtful treatment. Since the matter could not be resolved, it was submitted to Bishop Antonio Trivulzio as a kind of musical litigation.

Unfortunately, present-day scholars sometimes find themselves involved in discussions no less heated and controversial than those of Danckerts and his colleagues many centuries ago, and those with the time and inclination for reviewing ancient battles may learn as much about human beings as about *musica ficta* in the following articles: Edward E. Lowinsky, 'The Function of Conflicting Signatures in Early Polyphonic Music', *The Musical Quarterly* XXXI (1945), 227-260; Richard H. Hoppin, 'Partial Signatures and Musica Ficta in Some Early 15th-Century Sources', *Journal of the American Musicological Society* VI (1953), 197-215; Lowinsky, 'Conflicting Views on Conflicting Signatures', *JAMS* VII (1954), 181-204; Hoppin, 'Conflicting Signatures Reviewed', *JAMS* IX (1956), 97-117. When the dust has settled, it will be readily appreciated by those who have had the good fortune to consult musicians familiar with early repertoire that viewing such problems, and attempting to solve them by a purely theoretical or analytical approach, or (worst of all) by playing them on the piano, leads only to frustration and argument. The music must be heard in context: that is, it must be performed by the forces for which it was written. Then, and only then, can it be properly judged.

Examples abound in the richly-woven polyphonic tapestries of the Tudors, especially Tallis, Taverner, Fayrfax, Tye, and Byrd, to whom the false relation ('cross relation' in America) was a way of harmonic life. This massive close to the *Credo* of Taverner's Mass *Gloria tibi Trinitas* will sound ugly on a keyboard instrument, but when sung by a fine body of trained musicians it can warm the heart and chill the spine at one and the same moment:

Ex. 31

(Amen)

The most recent edition, however, is not necessarily the best. In the old *Tudor Church Music* edition (I, 144), the F marked with an asterisk is left natural, as it should be, echoing at a lower octave the outline of the falling phrase in the top line, previous bar. But in *Early English Church Music* (20, 45) that crucial and gorgeous dissonance is all but banished by means of a cautionary sharp. Of a recognizably similar cast is Ex. 32, a piquant cadence in the first strain of the dance-section of Monteverdi's *Il Ballo delle Ingrate*, which in several current editions is misrepresented by adding a sharp to the first violin's C in the penultimate bar. Yet the logic of contrary motion sustains it, as in the Taverner example, and those who know the final chorus of the *Ballo* will have no doubts about the plangent possibilities of such a device.*

* Perhaps the most remarkable *querelle des bouffons* in the entire history of the *musica ficta* controversy took place in 1973, as a result of a review in the *Times Literary Supplement* for June 29. A heated and lengthy correspondence ensued, staying its course for several months before petering out in a string of apologies, retractions and resignations. It can be said, however, that editions published since that storm in a teacup show signs of greater awareness in the random application of sharps, flats and naturals.

Ex. 32

Missing and Misplaced Parts

Mention of the *Ballo* also recalls the case of the missing second violin part, which provides so much of the harmonic spice in the suspensions that occur on many strong beats of the dance section. Not that the part was ever actually lost: it was simply overlooked by those who scored the work from the partbooks. Missing lines or sections sometimes cause a masterpiece to look more mutilated than it really is, as with the 'Winter' concerto in Vivaldi's *Four Seasons* which is sometimes bereft of its obbligato cello part. On the other hand some parts are optional, like the additional con-tratenors for Ciconia's *O felix templum* (1400) and Antonio Romano's *Stirps Mocenigo* (1414). When some-thing is obviously missing and should be supplied editori-ally because the harmony is incomplete, great care must be exercised in order to ensure that the additional material matches the composer's style to perfection. English schol-ars seem to have a knack for this kind of restoration, as witness the work on Byrd's *Great Service* by E.H. Fellowes, on the Eton Manuscript by Frank Harrison and on Gib-bons's verse anthems by David Wulstan.

A problem of a rather special nature is posed by the double choir *Magnificat* of Monteverdi's *Selva morale*

(Malipiero ed., XV, 639), for it was published without the alto and bass parts of choir 2. Despite the obvious imbalance of choral tone, the work has often been performed – and even recorded – as a six-part *Magnificat*. This disastrous procedure, against which even the humblest of choirmasters should have been warned by the odd appearance of the score, not only deprives choir 2 of half its body, but also demotes a duet for bass and baritone soloists to the sad status of a baritone solo, making nonsense of Monteverdi's formal design. Yet the bass part is comparatively easy to supply since the continuo bass outlines its shape with generous clarity:

Ex. 33

From Monteverdi's *Magnificat* for double-choir and orchestra, showing the duet for baritone and bass. By permission of Novello & Co. Ltd.

Also part of the close thicketed *Selva*, the first *Dixit Dominus* (XV, 195) is presented as a solid eight-part mass of polyphony, the editor remarking that although some voices bear the designation *secondo choro* no particular evidence of antiphony exists. This is true of the first three pages, but on the fourth (at 'Sede a dextris meis') the staggered entries point conclusively to a double-choir arrangement, confirmed even more clearly at 'inimicos tuos'. Incidentally this psalm reappears, in an inferior re-working (or more probably an earlier version) in the posthumously published *Messa . . . Salmi . . . Letanie* of 1650 (Malipiero ed., XVI, 54), where the double-choir layout is obvious despite the partly different music.*

The same inability to size up a dialogue situation has persuaded both scholars and musicians to regard Sweelinck's magnificent setting of *Diligam te Domine* (for the wedding of the composer Johann Stobaeus) as an eight-part motet for one choir. Once again, however, a keen glance at the published score (Seiffert ed., IX, 37) shows where each voice really belongs. This is also true of some secular dialogues in modern editions, such as Vicentino's *Amor, ecco ch' io moro*, where the seven voice-parts

*For a recent edition, see Claudio Monteverdi: *Christmas Vespers (Novello, London, 1979).*

185

require a certain amount of re-arrangement, or the Lasso setting of Ronsard's *Que dis-tu, que fais-tu?*, in which the four-part choir in the uppermost position is lower in tessitura than the 'second' choir. Careful and penetrating study of each new work will in most cases reveal the best way of interpreting its idiosyncrasies, bringing out its special features, and performing it in a manner that will highlight its form and style.

Barring

Many performers of early music continue to experience great difficulty in finding the correct tempo for vocal as well as instrumental works, and (what is even more important) the correct amount and frequency of stresses or accents – not in the sense of audible bumps, but rather of subliminary pulses, without which music cannot live and breathe. Much of this difficulty is due to editors, countless numbers of whom, with immense labour but insufficient musical thought, put part-books into score by ruling barlines at depressingly regular intervals and so 'box in' what is essentially a free-flowing complex of rising and falling lines with or without literary text. The effect on performers can often be extremely discouraging, and their only way of escape from this barred prison is to move the offending objects out of the way, or into another place.

Although much of the Renaissance repertoire looks after itself, it is still necessary to be watchful when homophony takes over and demands a sensible projection of the text. The same is true of some homophony that is polyphonically animated, such as this extract from Stoltzer's *Erzürne dich nicht*, cited in an excellent but little-known article on 'Editionstechnik' by Hans Albrecht (*Die Musik in Geschichte und Gegenwart* 3, cols. 1109-1146). Although the verbal stresses should be aided by musical ones, the word 'Gesetz' receives false accentuation, and the underlay of text to music is unsuitable and inconsistent here and there. Just as we accept the idea of musical homophony, so we should with words in those passages where words and syllables call for correct alignment in more than one voice-part (e.g. 'seines Gottes'):

Ex. 34(a)

Ex. 34(b)

Albrecht reminds us that there are three very good reasons for improving the way in which original texts were underlaid to notes: the scribes and printers were often inexact, they used repetition signs that frequently left matters entirely to the performer, and a modern edition should therefore try to solve these problems for the performer. Ex. 34b (opposite) shows my suggested revision.

It is no longer good enough to leave questions of macrorhythm to choir directors and instrumentalists, who rarely have the time to study the history and theory of musical notation as it evolved in the Middle Ages and the Renaissance – a subject too vast and complex even for many scholars. A harpsichordist or a dance ensemble keen to try out some of the dances in Francesco Bendusi's *Opera nova de balli à 4* (Venice, 1553) may be forgiven for assuming that 'Speranza' is a brisk two-in-a-bar (Ex. 35a) because of the time-signature and the usual manner of barring, when the underlying 'isorhythm' clearly pre-supposes (b) with the end result (c) shown on p. 190.

Ex. 35(a, b)

Ex. 35(c)

Certain rhythmical aspects of Bendusi's dance imply the feeling, if not the fact, of a hemiola; and this is so common a feature of Renaissance music – not to mention its frequent occurrence in later repertoire – that a well-prepared edition should reflect its presence. Reference is sometimes made to Giovanni Gabrieli's predilection for off-beat accents, and this certainly passes for a valid observation when his 8-part *Jubilate Deo* (1597) is barred as in Ex. 36a.

Ex. 36(a)

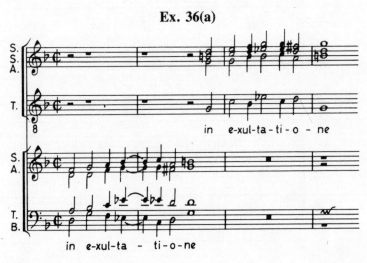

But the music and text make better sense when presented to the performer's eye as follows:

Ex 36(b)

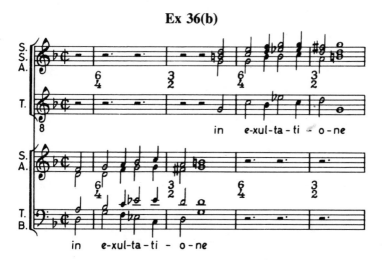

In most cases an immediate improvement in feeling and declamation can be achieved by a simple displacement of editorial bar-lines, so that the false accents of Ex. 37a (from Pallavicino's *Cruda Amarilli*, Book VI à 5) become sensible and correct as in Ex. 37b.

Ex. 37(a, b)

Aside from this displacement of bar-lines in duple time, the most frequent feature calling for recognition is the hidden tripla section, usually noticeable as a macro-rhythm $\frac{3}{1}$ or $\frac{3}{2}$ as in this extract from another Pallavicino madrigal, *Era l'anima mia*, from Book VI à 5:

Ex. 38(a, b)

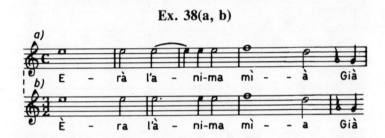

The tell-tale tie over a bar-line (Ex. 38a) ought to lead the reader's eye immediately to the source of trouble, and once this ability to recognize such situations has been fully developed, the problem of faulty accentuation will be banished. A macro-tripla involving a hemiola shift can be sensed in this madrigal by Gesualdo, *Che fai meco* (Book IV à 5):

Ex. 39(a)

Ex. 39(b)

For a discussion of some of the more troublesome passages in Monteverdi's madrigals, the reader is referred to the preface to my edition *Ten Madrigals for Mixed Voices* (O.U.P., 1978); and it should be borne in mind that equally treacherous passages occur in his religious music. In the *Laudate pueri* (first setting) in the *Selva morale* – Malipiero ed., XV, 438 – the section beginning 'Quis sicut Dominus' obscures the hemiola and the right declamation (Ex. 40a), though a slight adjustment restores the balance in a way that helps the performers (Ex. 40b):

Ex. 40(a)

Ex. 40(b)

In the final resort, it is the trained and practised eye that reveals the composer's true intent, so often sadly obfuscated by editorial sins of omission and commission; and one of the best ways to train and practise is to read through different editions of various composers with the aim and object of discovering what can be modified or improved.

Twelve
Problems in Literary Texts

> Do not you observe how excellently the
> ditty is affected in every place? That I do
> not marry a word of short quantity to a
> long note? Nor an ascending syllable to a
> descending tone?
>
> Ben Johnson: *Cynthia's Revels*

If the horrendous depth and frequent occurrence of musical pitfalls can bid fair to swallow up the unwary performer, the problems – visible and invisible – inherent in literary texts that go hand in hand with the music often seem no less daunting, even though capable of ultimate resolution. Unfortunately for music very few scholars are willing or able to take the time to correct obvious errors. More than one edition of the English *Alleluia psallat* (from the so-called Worcester Fragments) obliges the choir to sing about the 'happy blind man' ('*laetus caecus*') when they should be praising the happy throng ('*laetus cetus*'); and stranger phrases abound in longer motets, for numerous ancient scribes were poor Latinists, and modern transcribers either follow their nonsense, blindly but happily, or invent new oddities of their own through lack of experience in the field of palaeography. *Lux fulget ex Anglia*, like many other motets of the late Middle Ages, flaunts a text more corrupt than the Avignon papacy, yet once it is recognized as a work in honour of St Thomas of Hereford – not St Thomas of Canterbury – a little research into the rhymed offices of *Analecta Hymnica* XIII reveals a much more satisfactory and intelligible version (p. 248) than that of the Modena MS, Bibl. Estense, lat.471.

Latin texts tend to be more problematic than most for the simple reason that the somewhat shaggy language of the vast majority of non-liturgical motets has rarely attracted the undivided attention of skilled medievalists. The first modern edition of *Salve, cara Deo tellus* by the 15th-century composer Lodovico da Rimini appeared as long ago as 1934, but it was not until 1942 that the poem was recognized to be one of Petrarch's metrical epistles (*Rivista Musicale Italiana*, XLVI, pp. 65-78). Even then, no attempt was made to fit a reliable text of the poem to the extant music of Trent MS. 87, a source not particularly noted for its general trustworthiness. Indeed, as may be seen from the following text, in which italicized words show a superior reading to the footnoted Trent versions, the errors and omissions are by no means few.*

Salve, cara Deo tellus *sanctissima*, salve
tellus tuta bonis, tellus metuenda superbis.
tellus nobilibus multum generosior oris,
fertilior cunctis, terra formosior *omni*,
5 *cincta* mari gemino, *famoso* splendida monte,
armorum legumque eadem veneranda sacrarum
Pieridumque domus auroque opulenta virisque,
cuius ad eximios ars et natura favores
incubuere simul mundoque dedere magistram.
10 Ad te nunc cupide post tempora longa revertor
incola perpetuus: tu diversoria vite
grata dabis fesse, tu *quantum* pallida tandem
membra *tegant prestabis humum*. Te letus ab alto
Italiam *video frondentis colle* Gebenne.
15 Nubila post tergum remanent; ferit ora serenus
spiritus et *blandis* assurgens *motibus* aer
excipit. Agnosco *patriam gaudensque* saluto:
salve, *pulchra* parens, terrarum gloria, salve.

Notes: line 1 sacratissima; 1.3 *omitted*; 1.4 ori; 1.5 cuncto, fecunda; 1.5 armorumque legum, eadem *omitted*; ll.6-7 transposed: 1.7 pyeridum mater auro; 1.8 huius; 1.9 incumbere; 1.12 grata *omitted*, quartum: 1.13 te gratiam prestas humani; 1.14 videam frondentem monte; 1.16 gratus, montibus; 1.17 gaudens patriamque; 1.18 sancta.

*A corrected version of both music and text is published by Novello & Co., 1974.

Such instances could be multiplied at will, and quite apart from Latin texts there are French, Italian, German, English, Spanish and other languages to be taken into account. The performer, should he have cause to mistrust the edition he is using, has one line of recourse only – to an expert in the field of language to which the work belongs.

Right or wrong, the literary text can pose other thorny questions, especially when it is obviously incomplete and no concordance exists to fill the gap. A well-known song by Binchois, *Filles à marier*, got itself into print and on record not once but many times before the full text became familiar. Although there is no musical concordance for Binchois, a different setting of the poem in the Seville Chansonnier shows that the earlier composition must be provided with the following lines in order to make good sense and plausible *ballade* form:

> Filles à marier,
> Ne vous mariez ja,
> Se bien vous ne scavez
> Quel mary vous prendra.
>
> Car se jalousie a,
> Jamez ne vous ne luy
> Au cueur joye n'ara,
> Et pour ce pensez y.

This correction was made by Dragan Plamenac in his thorough-going article 'A Reconstruction of the French Chansonnier in the Biblioteca Columbina, Seville', *The Musical Quarterly* XXXVII (1951), 519, but when Wolfgang Rehm's edition of the Binchois chansons was completed four years later (and published in 1957) the song still had an incomplete text and no proper classification as regards its form. For a particularly valuable study of this topic, see Nino Pirrotta, 'On Text Forms from Ciconia to Dufay', in *Aspects of Medieval and Renaissance Music: a Birthday Offering to Gustave Reese* (New York, 1966), 673-682.

Another disguised *ballade* came to light, belatedly but brilliantly, in a classic study by David Fallows, 'English Song Repertories of the Mid-fifteenth Century', *Proceedings of the Royal Musical Association* 103 (1976/77), 61-79, in which the strange history of Bedingham's *Gentil madona* is engagingly recounted. Two things about it invited suspicion: the uneasy fit of the Italian poem to the *ballade* form of the song, and the existence of several concordances beginning with *Fortune, Fortuna las,* or *Fortune elas*. Dr Fallows looked for an English poem in *ballade* stanzas with just such an incipit and found that a 15th-century lyric known to scholars of English literature since at least 1909 suited the music to perfection:

> Fortune alas, alas, what have I gylt
> In prison thus to lye here desolate?

As in the case of the Petrarch-Rimini song, underlaying a correct text made for a happier marriage with the melody, as well as restoring one more little gem to the song repertoire.

The effects of such an operation, but on a large-scale basis, can best be seen in a still outstanding and admirable contribution to American scholarship, Helen Hewitt's edition of Petrucci's *Harmonice Musices Odhecaton A* (Cambridge, Mass., 1942). Here is an old song-book from the very cradle of music-printing, a precious repository of polyphonic music (for the most part secular, with French texts predominant), but largely unusable on account of the fact that lyrics are complete only in very few instances. Most of the pieces are provided with an incipit only, for the exact underlay of text to music was a difficult and time-consuming process even for the ingenious Petrucci who had perfected techniques of multiple-impression printing. Moreover he evidently assumed, with some justification, that the majority of performers would either know the song-texts by heart or would have access to them in some printed collection or manuscript commonplace book.

It would have been relatively simple to transcribe the

music and incipits as Petrucci had printed them, offering readers the shabby excuse that nothing in scholarship is more noble than to respect the authority of the source. Instead, Dr Hewitt, working in close collaboration with Isabel Pope, diligently traced the texts in other musical manuscripts, polyphonic and monophonic, and even found six of them in literary sources unrelated to music. The recovered texts, amounting to more than three-quarters of the *Odhecaton*, were then carefully underlaid to the music in such a way as to breathe new life into a skeletal repertoire. In the words of Dr Hewitt:

> It would, indeed, have been a curious thing if Petrucci, in printing such a bulk of music, the sum total of his publication of secular art works by Netherlanders, a cross section of the finest secular polyphonic artworks composed in his day and representative of the best work of a school of writers famous for their vocal polyphony, had had the intention that these compositions, many of them known to be vocal in conception, should be performed on instruments. . . . The editorial policy regarding texts, therefore, has been to introduce into the transcriptions such texts as have been found in contemporary sources.

As we have seen in earlier chapters of this book, each historical epoch presents its repertoire in a manner that would have been easily grasped by performers of the time, but not necessarily by those of our own age. Thus it is essential to understand the medieval liturgy to complete texts of which the plainsong element was omitted; it is helpful to know the principles of Renaissance instrumentation in order to add the requisite colour to songs, motets, and occasional pieces; it is desirable to become acquainted with poetry of the 15th and 16th centuries if the music using that poetry is to make proper sense;* and in the era of the thorough-bass it is incumbent upon the performer to

---

*A useful anthology is that edited by Brian Jeffery, *Chanson Verse of the Early Renaissance* (London, 1971).

realize the harmonic implications of the basses and their figures (if any) so as to allow the music to achieve its full impact and effectiveness. The true scholar and editor must always be prepared to add to what he finds, even though the old saying *inventis facile est addere* may sometimes sound like an understatement.

Not all missing texts are poetical, however, for although the prose text is fairly rare in music it cannot be entirely ruled out as a possibility for a solution to a mysterious incipit. Editing *The Mulliner Book* for Musica Britannica in 1951, I succeeded in tracing a number of poems that fitted the keyboard reductions of what were obviously part-songs from the mid-16th century, such as *My friends* (Earl of Surrey, after Martial), *I smile to see how you devise* and *When griping griefs* (Edwards), and others of the same kind drawing on lyrics from the Elizabethan miscellanies. It did not prove difficult to expand these versions into open score so as to make the music viable once again for vocal quartet. Nevertheless, a few incipits proved elusive, though the complete poems came to light in subsequent years and the repertoire of part songs steadily grew larger.

One piece by Tallis, beginning *O ye tender babes*, defeated me at first because it stubbornly refused to show up in the collections of verse, both manuscript and printed, where I had expected to find it. Eventually I found it quite by accident in William Lily's *An Introduction to the Eyght Partes of Speche* published in 1540. This was an elementary Latin grammar which led on to a more detailed textbook in Latin entitled *Institutio Compendiaria Totius Grammaticae*, both parts being intended for schoolboys in the earliest stages of their education. The work is introduced by a lengthy address to schoolmasters, fathers of families, and lastly the pupils themselves:

> You tender babes of Englande, shake off slouthfulness, set wantonnes a parte, apply your wyttes holy to learnyng and vertue, whereby you may doo youre duetye to god and your kyng, make gladde your

> parentes, profytte your selues, and moche auaunce the common weale of your countrey.

This admonitory piece of prose, when underlaid to the music of Thomas Tallis, fits so convincingly that there is no need to doubt the concern of the composer for the well being of the 'babes' who might have sung the treble part as a musical offering at morning prayers.*

The art of extracting and editing texts from early sources goes back well beyond the 16th century, and as a general rule it can be stated that the earlier the poem, the more difficult it is to deal with. But there are always exceptions, and those who find themselves fascinated by the special kind of detective work associated with early texts should not fail to read an article by Dragan Plamenac, 'On Reading Fifteenth-Century Chanson Texts', *Journal of the American Musicological Society* XXX (1977), 320-324. Discussing chansons by Ockeghem, Dr Plamenac observes that *Se vostre cueur* is found with text only in one source (the Pixérécourt manuscript) so that problem words and phrases have to be worked out by the editor. No copy of the poem as a separate entity has so far come to light. Fortunately the first three lines make perfect sense:

> Se vostre cueur eslongne de moy a tort
> Et que de vous je n'ay(e) plus confort,
> Je prendray lors sur Dieu et sur mon ame . . .

But the last two, as copied by the scribe, seem to defy decoding – one line is obviously corrupt, while the other lacks two syllables:

> Que ce mon deuous ne frome res ame
> Qui mains vous voulsit faire tort.

Happily Dr Plamenac was able to bring to bear on this difficult couplet his considerable knowledge not only of palaeography but also of old French vocabulary and

---

*See 'A Musical Admonition for Tudor Schoolboys', *Music & Letters* 38 (1957), 49-52, where there is a reconstruction of the song.

grammar, realizing that the abbreviation beginning with *q* should read *qu'en*, that *mon* and *de* should be combined, and that *frome res* is a scribal error for *trouverés*, since *f* and *t* are often confused, as are *m, n, u, v*. As for the missing syllables, he surmised that they probably occurred at a change of line where the scribe copied words beginning with *q* and *m* only once when they should have appeared twice. His brilliant reconstruction of the last two lines reads as follows:

> Qu'en ce monde vous ne trouverés ame
> Qui mains que moy vous voulsit faire tort.

> *If your heart should wrongly retire from me*
> *And if I should have no further comfort from you,*
> *I shall then take it on God and on my soul*
> *That in this world you will not find a soul*
> *Who would wish to wrong you less than I.*

Extracting texts from polyphony in order to present the poem in its correct form can sometimes lead to trouble unless proper account is taken of the reverse process – when the composer breaks up verse into suitable pieces for underlaying to music. If you take Dufay's *La dolce vista* as it stands in the Vatican manuscript Urb. lat. 1411 (the unique source) and copy out the text it would look as follows:

La dolce vista	O lieta faccia
La dolce vista	o Lieta faça
del tuo viso pio	o rosa
conforta donna	o rosa colorita
conforta donna	fra tutti laltri
conforta donna	ti dono el cor mio.
sempre el me desio.	

Deprived of the repetitions, and with some punctuation added, the verse emerges as four lines of the usual eleven syllables each:

> La dolce vista del tuo viso pio
> conforta, donna, sempre el me desio.
> O lieta faccia, O rosa colorita,
> fra tutti l'altri ti dono el cor mio.

In his Sixth Book of Madrigals (1614) Monteverdi sets Scipione Agnelli's *Incenerite spoglie* for five voices as a memorial to the singer Caterina Martinelli, but in doing so he sometimes introduces a phrase in such a way as to 'bend' the rather rigid form – *sestina* – in which the poem is cast. Copied out exactly from the music, verse 1 would read:

> Incenerite spoglie, avara tomba,
> fatta del mio bel Sol, terreno Cielo;
> ahi lasso, i' vegno ad inchinarvi in terra,
> con voi chiuso è 'l mio cor a marmi in seno,
> e notte e giorno vive in pianto, in foco,
> in duolo, in ira il tormentato Glauco.

The other verses confirm that the six words that must end each line in this *sestina* are 'tomba', 'Cielo', 'terra', 'seno', 'pianto', and 'Glauco'; so the last two lines should be re-arranged to read:

> e notte e giorno vive in foco, in pianto,
> in duolo, in ira il tormentato Glauco.

Further adjustment is necessary at the end of verse 2, because the last word of each verse must re-appear as the final word of the first line in the succeeding verse. Thus, despite the musical setting, the verse should end in this way:

> a me fu cibo il duol, bevanda il pianto;
> letto, o sasso felice, il tuo bel seno,
> poich' il mio ben coprì gelida terra.

Certain verse forms, of less regular type, nevertheless create patterns of their own which should be deduced from the overall picture. Jacopo Peri's *Tu dormi*, a masterpiece of early through-composed monody, is based on a poem that might seem disorganized as regards its rhyme and metre if extracted loosely in accordance with the musical cadences:

> Tu dormi, e 'l dolce sonno ti lusinga con l'ali
> Aure volanti ne mov' ombra giammai, taci li pianti.
> Io, che non ho riposo
> Se non quando da lumi verso torrent' e fiumi,
> esc' a notturno sol, a me gioioso . . .

When the juxtaposition of lines having either seven or eleven syllables is fully grasped, the structure of the verse becomes clear at once:

Tu dormi, e 'l dolce sonno	a	7
ti lusinga con l'ali, aure volanti;	b	11
ne mov' ombra giammai, taci li pianti.	b	11
Io, che non ho riposo	c	7
se non quando da lumi	d	7
verso torrent' e fiumi,	d	7
esc' al notturno sol, a me gioioso.	c	11
Tu lo splendor degl' argentati rai	e	11
non rimiri, e tu stai	e	7
sord' al duol che m'accora;	f	7
io sent' e veggio ogn'or l'aura e l'aurora.	f	11

Alertness to a rhyme scheme helps to make sense in all languages, even Greek, as may be seen in this final section from a wedding dialogue by Christoph Demantius (*Das Erbe Deutscher Musik*, Sonderreihe, Band 1, 1939):

Votum annectemus?	Demus.
Revalete,	Valete.
Adsit ἔρως,	Heros.
Dira fugeris,	ἔρως.
Fata huic qui thalamo	
meditantur iniqua potenter	
frange, Jehova, viros.	Ange, Jehova, viros.

The typical dialogue or echo technique shortens the last word of every phrase as it is sung by the second choir, but the editor overlooked the important fact that the second ἔρως must be ἔρις in order to rhyme:

Shall we make the vow firm?	Let us do so.
Be strong,	Be healthy.
May Love be with us,	A hero.
May you escape all harm,	Strife.
O Jehovah, shatter with your power the men who contemplate evil for this marriage-bed.	Make them suffer, O Jehovah.

Underlay of Text

One of the most critical and crucial of many editorial and performance problems – the matter of underlaying text convincingly to a series of notes – ranks with *musica ficta* as a top priority for investigation. But no monograph has so far appeared; and of two extant dissertations one is restricted to Dufay's Masses while the other discusses only 16th century liturgical music with English texts. The early theorists contribute a superabundance of verbose confusion, borrowing rules, changing them, adding to them, and then making exceptions to them; while the modern scholar tries to deal with the situation as best he can, never sure that his flashes of insight will reach the people who need it most of all. One good sign is that more early material is coming to light, and even though little of it can lay claim to novelty, certain information both positive and negative can assist us in trying to understand a somewhat complex and debatable aspect of performance practice.

The anonymous author of what is at present thought to be the earliest piece of advice about underlay – a single leaf of instructions written in northern Italy about 1440 – begins with this splendid statement:

Be it known that there is absolutely no rhyme or reason in having to put words properly to notes other than the mind of him who has to write it down.

The remainder of this brief treatise, probably written by a

choir director for one of his assistants or pupils, is devoted
to the fairly obvious: sing the syllable to the note under
which it is placed, and keep on singing the vowel until
another syllable comes along. The entire matter is exhaustively discussed in an article by Don Harrán, 'In Pursuit of
Origins: The Earliest Writing on Text Underlay', Acta
Musicologica L (1978), 217-240. The responsible person is
the composer or copyist, neither of them free from occasional blame (if we are to believe Vicentino, of whom
more anon), so that the singer can either do what he is told
or invent something better. Gilbert Reaney, investigating
'Text Underlay in Early Fifteenth-Century Musical
Manuscripts', In *Essays in Musicology in Honor of Dragan
Plamenac* (Pittsburgh, 1969), points out that in the upper
parts of a composition

> the text is usually present, but unfortunately it is never
> placed exactly as it should be: in other words, even
> very accurate manuscripts do not place all the syl-
> lables exactly under the notes to which they must be
> sung.

In other words there is no such thing as total reliability, and
little point in trying to invent and observe hard-and-fast
rules. Edward Lowinsky, in his Introduction to Helen
Hewitt's edition of *Canti B Numero Cinquanta* (Chicago,
1967), deplores such barbarisms in modern publications as
the interruption of one word by the rest, and the holding of
one syllable over repeated notes, footnoting the fact that
the interruption syndrome was, in earlier periods – the
trecento, for example – part of the physiognomy of its vocal
style.

Taking a broad view of the question, however, it does
seem odd that editors should be blamed for following too
closely the vagaries of 15th-century scribes, whereas those
of the 13th century should escape scot-free because the
fault is said to lie with the vocal techniques of the age.
Could not both be due to one and the same thing – the
human element in manuscript production? It is a well-

known fact that the more costly manuscripts were produced by at least three scribes, one looking after
illuminated initials, while the other two concentrated on
music and text respectively. Even when the same man
wrote both music and text, the possibility of error was
considerable since he was no better than his source-
material, which in turn may have been second-hand or
worse.

If Italy is acknowledged to be one of the most important
musical centres in the Middle Ages, as much for composers
as for singers – whose voices, though silent now, surely live
on in some of the great Italian artists of our own day – then
surely a piece of vocal nonsense like the opening of Jacopo
da Bologna's *Non al suo amante* should never be tolerated
by modern editors, no matter what the manuscripts say?

Ex. 41

Would any sane singer, ancient or modern, sing the first
word 'Non' with three pauses for breath before going on to
the next word? Where would he put the second 'n' of 'Non'
– on the final triplet quaver of bar 5? And even if this were
possible, would it sound artistic and convincing?

The sad fact is that the wonderful vocal repertory of the
Italian trecento, full of glittering gems worthy of perfect
settings, has now been 'edited' several times in various
different series of publications, but each time with the same
musical result, a fair example of which is given as Ex. 41.
Can nothing be done to improve matters? Returning to the

Lowinsky Introduction cited earlier, we find the following observation:

> The practice of spreading a number of syllables more or less evenly over long melismas obstructs the understanding of the words; it can often be successfully replaced by pulling the sentence together at the beginning of the melodic phrase and placing the melismas at the end of the textual phrase. Accentuation can be improved in many cases, although it will hardly ever be perfect, at least not before the second half of the sixteenth century.

These are wise words, whose basic principle is followed not only in the exemplary edition of *Canti B* but also in *The Medici Codex* (Chicago, 1968), and there is no reason why that principle should not be followed in the music of earlier times. Jacopo's setting, as usually performed after the example of modern editors, would have shocked Petrarch if he could hear how his madrigal text had been mangled. But a slight re-adjustment of text to music produces much better sense and is infinitely more pleasing to singer and listener alike:

Ex. 42

Admittedly, this is not in strict accord with the rules of Vicentino or Zarlino, but is there any reason why it should be, considering the centuries that separate them from Jacopo da Bologna? I suggest that the time has now come for a new approach to text-underlay in medieval music – an approach that will help to remove barbarisms in declamation and sense even though there are no 'rules' so far discovered to tell us exactly what composers wanted from their singers. Whatever they wanted, it certainly was not nonsense.

This is not to say that oddities cannot emerge in special situations. Occasionally an instrumental line, devoid of text in one source, is almost submerged in it elsewhere; and the technique of adding text consisted apparently of breaking long notes into shorter ones and squeezing in as many words as possible. This is what happens in the case of Reson's *Salve Regina,* edited by Gilbert Reaney in vol. 2 of his series 'Early Fifteenth-Century Music' (Rome, 1959). Of the two extant sources, both in Bologna, only the manuscript at the University Library gives text to the tenor part. A texted contratenor would be out of the question since the line is so agile and angular that vocal performance rules itself out. But the tenor has been adapted as follows:

Ex. 43

Admittedly, that is not the most subtle and sensitive example of underlay, but it serves its purpose – a purely functional one, presumably, and its position guarantees at least partial inaudibility.

This is not so in certain songs whose only text lies in the upper voice, or where all voices veer towards the homophonic. One of Dufay's best known compositions, *Vergine bella*, has frequently appeared in print and on record with faulty accentuation as early as the first two lines (a), which can easily be corrected (b) if the editor or singer takes the trouble to read the poem out loud:

Ex. 44(a, b)

Comparable quirks often spoil the close of Josquin's *El grillo*, which though generally edited and sung as in (a), is susceptible of improvement as in (b), which respects both sense and accentuation while making for a happier marraige of text and music:

Ex. 45(a, b)

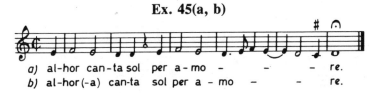

In the absence of rules the musician should make his own choice, for he will find little or no direct assistance in theorists such as Gafori, and the earliest helpful treatise in the 16th century comes on the scene only in 1553, when Giovanni Maria Lanfranco – more a practical man than a pure theorist – published his *Scintille di musica* as an aid to choirboys and others desirous of elementary musical training. Lanfranco must have been witness to a long tradition, for his rules are so clear and to the point that Zarlino made copious use of them in his *Istitutioni harmoniche* of 1558*

---

* Zarlino's rules are most easily accessible in the translation by Oliver Strunk, *Source Readings in Music History* (New York, 1950), 259.

as has been skilfully revealed by Don Harrán in his 'New Light on the Question of Text Underlay prior to Zarlino', *Acta Musicologica* XLV (1973), 24-56. But for real brevity and clarity we should turn to Nicola Vicentino's *L'antica musica ridotta all moderna prattica* (Rome, 1555), where he makes composers and singers jointly responsible for barbarisms (chapter XXX, fol. 86v-87). According to him, some singers repeat syllables and words when no such repetition is indicated, and some composers repeat words pointlessly. Other composers occasionally leave out words, and so the singers cannot underlay the text properly. He feels that all should recognize the fact that when the music has more notes than syllables, and many notes (even crotchets and quavers) have to be sung to one syllable, the next syllable should *not* be placed on the first white note following the black notes, but on the second, no matter whether the line ascends or descends. His example sums up the matter succinctly:

Ex. 46

Regola uniuerfale di porre le parole fotto alle note.

Gaudea   mus om   nes in do   mino diem   fe   flum

non buona pronuntia.

di em fe flum   diem feflum si pronuntia la fillaba fotto la nera per bifogno.

An excellent account of the theory and practice of text-underlay in the Medici Codex (1518) is given in the Historical Introduction to Edward Lowinsky's edition (Chicago, 1968), 90-107; and much of this information can also be applied to contemporaneous manuscripts and printed editions. Vicentino's complaints about useless repetitions must yield occasionally to a common-sense attitude that would avoid an even worse solecism: the interruption of a musical phrase in the middle of a word, and this attitude is recommended by Lowinsky for certain passages such as the following, from Mouton's *Salva nos, Domine*:

Ex. 47

Some solutions are less convincing because they stem from a too close adherence to the modern bar-line, thrust into the flow of the voices at every fourth crotchet and creating feelings of stress and syncopation undreamed of by the composer. According to Lowinsky (p. 106):

> The character of a syncopated note springs from its ambiguous play between pull and stress. This ambiguity is lost when the syncopated note receives a syllable. Observing this where we can – like most other rules in this period it suffers exceptions – we may even arrive at a better solution in a work so unsatisfactory from the point of view of text underlay as Josquin's *Miserere*:

Ex. 48

213

But in rhythmic notation the second version reveals its
inadequacies (a), which could be improved as in (b) and
underlaid as in (c), where the unjustly convicted music is
finally free from its imprisoning bars:

Ex. 49(a, b, c)

As Sir Thomas Beecham was wont to tell his musicians:
'Forget about bars. Look at the phrases, please. Remember
that bars are only the boxes in which music is packed'.

It is a sad reminder of the tolerance or lack of concern on
the part of performers and editors when egregious errors
are cheerfully perpetuated from one edition to the next,
nobody bothering to correct them. Cipriano de Rore's
delicious madrigal *Dalle belle contrade* was edited long ago
with the word 'fruiva' set as a two-syllable word, and that is
the way it is generally performed – (a), when (b) is obviously what Rore wanted:

Ex. 50(a)

214

Ex. 50(b)

Monteverdi's setting of Petrarch's *Zefiro torna* (Book VI) usually suffers faulty underlay (soprano) making gibberish of the poetical metre while the line is hard to sing (a), but once a slight adjustment has been made the flow becomes natural and the stress-pattern regular (b):

Ex. 51(a, b)

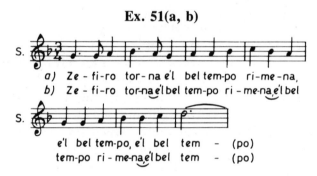

Zarlino's teaching, certainly known to Monteverdi (who owned a copy of the *Istitutioni harmoniche* and wrote his name on the title-page),* spread to Spain where Francisco de Salinas instructed, among others, a German musician and humanist, Kaspar Stocker, the author of a manuscript treatise *De musica verbali*. This is extensively analysed and discussed by Edward Lowinsky in 'A Treatise on Text Underlay by a German Disciple of Francisco de Salinas', in *Festschrift Heinrich Besseler* (Leipzig, 1961), 231-251. Stocker goes beyond Zarlino's rules, adding new material either invented by him or taken over from his teacher;

*See the facsimile in Gustave Reese, *Music in the Renaissance* (New York, 1954), plate IV.

Applied Musicology

furthermore he gives evidence of a broader sense of history than either the Italian or the Spaniard, for he is concerned to stress the difference between the age of Josquin and that of Willaert as exemplified in subtle variations of underlay technique. The old style permits two-note melismas, for instance, in a series of semiminims (crotchets), whereas the modern style allows only one syllable for the entire series.

Outside Italy one finds little in the way of instruction, though Thomas Morley, in his *Plaine and Easie Introduction to Practicall Musicke* (1597), writes persuasively of certain basic principles of underlay in the section dealing with 'Rules to be observed in dittying' (edition by R. Alec Harman, London 1952), 290. His main exhortation to the singer is to avoid false quantities:

> that we cause no syllable which is by nature short be expressed by many notes or one long note, nor no long syllables be expressed with a short note. But in this fault do the practitioners err more grossly than in any other, for you shall find few songs wherein the penult syllables of these words 'Dominus', 'Angelus', 'Filius', 'miraculum', 'gloria', and such like are not expressed with a long note, yea many times with a whole dozen of notes, and though one should speak of forty he should not say much amiss, which is a gross barbarism and yet might be easily amended.

Morley's cadence may serve as a sound piece of advice to musicians, echoing as it does a phrase in Hermann Finck's *Musica Practica* (1556), where the author rightly insists that

> in polyphonic music, in contrast to plainsong, the text is not really underlaid but simply appears beneath the notes in a general way. It is for the performers to decide exactly where the various syllables go.

So, dear performers, it is for you to decide – but try to do so with forethought, intelligence, and (above all) good taste.

Acknowledgements

The author and publishers are grateful to the following copyright owners for permission to include literary or musical quotations:

The Society of Authors on behalf of the Bernard Shaw Estate; Sir Thomas Beecham, Bt. and the Hutchinson Publishing Group Limited (*A Mingled Chime* and *Frederick Delius*, by Sir Thomas Beecham); Faber and Faber Limited (*The Letters of Monteverdi*); G. Henle Verlag (*RISM* B IV, 1); Professor H. Proctor-Gregg (*Sir Thomas Beecham*); Oxford University Press (*Monteverdi: Ten Madrigals*); Novello & Co. Ltd. (*Monteverdi: Magnificat for Double Choir*); The Governing Body of Christ Church, Oxford (*Sarum Antiphoner*); The Bodleian Library, Oxford (Lat.liturg.d.20).

Every reasonable effort has been made to contact copyright owners, but in the event of errors or omissions in the above list a correction will be made in subsequent printings of this book.

Index

Index

Index

Jeffery, Brian, 200n
Johnson, Dr Samuel,
  on 'second knowledge', 15
Jonson, Ben,
  Cynthia's Revels, 196
Josquin des Préz, 7, 51, 96, 151, 216
  collected editions, 75
  Déploration d'Ockeghem, 178–9,
    180
  El grillo, 211
  Miserere, 213–14
*Journal of the American Musical
  Instruments Society,* 146
*Journal of the American Musicological
  Society,* 38, 67, 80, 136, 155, 181,
  202

Kinsky, Georg, 41
Kirkpatrick, Ralph, 51
Köchel, Ludwig, 41
Krohn, Ernst C., 14
Krüger, Walter, 144
Kuhlau, Friedrich, 56

La Musica – Dizionario, 16
Lafontaine, H.C. de, 68
Landon, H.C. Robbins, 173
Lanfranco, Giovanni Maria, 211
Larousse de la Musique, 23
Lasso, Orlando di,
  setting of Ronsard's *Que dis-tu,
    que fais-tu?,* 186
Legrant, Guillaume,
  Credo, 150
Lehmann, Henri, 93
Lesure, François, 31
Lily, William, 201–2
Liszt, Franz, 91
Liturgy and music, 100–18
  further problems of form, 110–18
Llorens, José, 153
Lockspeiser, Edward, 45
Lockwood, Lewis, 181
Lowinsky, Edward E., 36, 67, 179,
  181, 207, 209, 212–3
Lux fulget ex Anglia, 196
Luzio, Alessandro, 152

McArdle, Donald, 69
MacClintock, Carol, 50, 132, 155
Machaut, Guillaume de, 73, 174, 175,
  178
  Mass, 145
Maeterlinck, Maurice, 70
Maffei, Giovanni Camillo, 127–8

Maldéghem, R.J. van, 72
Mancini, Giovanni Battista,
  *Riflessioni pratiche sul canto
    figurato,* 136
Masque of Flowers, The, 158–9
Marotta, Cesare, 68
Martinelli, Caterina, 204
Martini, G.B., 12
Martini, Padre, 170
Matteo da Perugia, 81–4
Maximilian I, 150
Maxwell Davies, Peter, 98
Medieval Academy of America, 62
Medici, Ferdinando de', 153
Melone, Annibale, 154
Mendel, Arthur, 176
Mendelssohn, 91, 93
  on ornamentation, 139–40
Menuhin, Yehudi,
  Music Guides, 4
  Musicology vs. Performance, 3
  Violin and Viola (with William
    Primrose), 154n
Messisbugo, Christoforo di, 152–3
MGG, 16
  on Bach, 75
  on collected works, 74, 75
  on music catalogues, 33–4
  on periodicals, 61
Mischiati, Oscar, 38
Monteverdi, Claudio, 7, 51, 172, 177,
  215
  Arianna, 60, 163
  Christmas Vespers, 185n
  *Combattimento di Tancredi e
    Clorinda,* 58, 60, 132
  Dixit Dominus, 60, 185
  Gloria Concertata a 7, 95n
  Il Ballo delle Ingrate, 130, 131n,
    182, 183
  Letters of, 58–60
  L'Orfeo, 60, 96, 97, 156
  Magnificats, 101, 108–10, 185
  Ritorno d'Ulisse, 93
  Selva morale, 183–4, 185, 194
  Zefiro torna, 58, 215
Monumenta Monodica Medii Aevi,
  104, 106
Morella, Giovanni Battista, 135
Morley, Thomas, 12, 216
Moskowa, Prince de la, 93
Mouton, Jean,
  Salva nos, domine, 213
Mozart, Wofgang Amadeus, 55, 93,
  160

221

DATE DUE